Best

Flossie

Audrey Sayre Hartley

"Thresh" Machine A Comin'
Memories of Jackson County
By
Audrey Sayre Hartley

Dedicated to the memory of
"That handsome neighbor boy",
Edward C. Hartley
1918-2006

International Standard Book Number 0-87012-782-9
Library of Congress Control Number 2008911241
Printed in the United States of America
Copyright © by Audrey Sayre Hartley
Cottageville, West Virginia
All Rights Reserved
2009

McClain Printing Company
Parsons, WV
www.mcclainprinting.com
2009

Cover photo: Author's home, Cow Run Valley.

On Valentine's Day, 2004, The *Parkersburg News* sponsored a contest asking for stories about "my first date". The author won a $200 gift certificate for the following story.

Love at First Sight...Or Not?

My first date was many many years ago and involved a skunk!

I was in my early teens in the 1930's and we lived in the country in Cow Run valley. It was winter and horses and wagons churned the red, clay, mud roads into an almost impassable consistency. Cars were put away for the winter and if you went anywhere, you walked but not on the roads. Even the ugly, over the shoe, high top galoshes we all wore then were no match for the sticky, red, clay mud. So we walked on paths, through cow pastures, that led from farm to farm.

One night a handsome neighbor boy asked me to join him on a walk to visit friends. Carrying a kerosene lantern, we made our way through the fields, occasionally crawling through a barbed wire fence. Everything was fine but then we met a skunk! To my dismay, the boy quickly captured the animal, catching and carrying it by the tail. He told me that in order to activate his scent gland a skunk must get his forefeet against something, so as long as you dangle it by the tail and don't let it touch anything, you are safe.

As an example of the depression times then, the boy's family paid their hired hand seventy-five cents a day plus two meals. So a number-one skunk skin, number one meaning all black, worth five dollars, was a big deal. However, there weren't many number ones. Most were two or threes, the price dropping lower with the amount of white on the skunk. Number fours were mostly white and worth very little.

We continued on, me, that boy and the skunk. Our friends were somewhat surprised that we had a skunk with us but quickly got a burlap bag to put him in.

We didn't meet any skunks on the way home that night, but I'm sure if we had, the skunk in the burlap bag would have had a companion.

I sometimes think of that first date and smile because that handsome neighbor boy and I just celebrated our 62nd wedding anniversary.

Thanks for your memories:

Herbert Sayre
Ralph Sayre
Frank and Ada Ruth Sayre
Hazel Hughes Sayre
Ruth Grady Smith
Park Shinn
Helen Gatchel Lester
Eugene McClure
Howard and Artist Taylor

The Great Depression

Times were hard in Cow Run Valley in the thirties, compounded by the terrible drought. Like other farming communities, I don't think anyone actually went hungry. Everyone had a garden, some chickens, a truck patch and probably a milk cow. I remember daddy using a sled and horses to haul barrels of water from Cow Run to do the weekly wash.

Cities and towns were desperate. There were some bread lines but a lot of people went hungry. A neighbor, Howard Taylor, who lived in St. Albans, told me he was nine years old and that three days was the longest he could remember going without anything to eat. Sometimes, hobos, camped down by the railroad tracks would give them a little food.

When people are hungry they will steal. Mom woke me late one night when she couldn't get daddy awake. She kept saying, "John, John someone is in the chickens". Most farm families owned a 22 rifle and a shotgun of some sort but we never did. On her last visit, my Aunt Minnie had brought a Smith and Wesson 32 revolver and asked Mom to keep it for her. She had had a break- in at her Charleston apartment. She was afraid it would happen again and she didn't want her gun stolen. With Mom carrying Aunt Minnie's revolver and me following close behind, we crept out along the garden fence toward the chicken house. Every few seconds we could hear a chicken go squaaaaaaaak" as it was caught. Mom stood up and fired twice and we heard footsteps running away. I don't know how my genteel mother knew how to load and fire that gun. I was about ten at the time and I remember that from then on the chicken house was padlocked at night. I also remember playing around the courthouse in Ripley, wandering into the courtroom and listening to the trial in progress that was about someone stealing chickens!

Ruth Grady's father was a minister and they lived in Parkersburg during the depression. They had a patch of corn that people were stealing. One night without her family's knowledge, Ruth slipped quietly out of the house carrying a double barrel shotgun. Taking a rest against the corner of the house, she fired. The men in the corn patch yelled "Don't shoot, don't shoot we're leaving!" Some days later when Ruth was walking to high school there were some men loitering on the street and she overheard one say to another "There goes that preacher's gal, watch out she'll shoot you!" Late one evening Ruth's mother went to the cellar to lock it. When the family heard her screams they found her lying on the ground. She had been knocked down and ran over by a man who came rushing out of the cellar. Later they found a bucket of lard he had dropped. Ruth's family was like everybody's--they were hard up. The toes were out of Ruth's shoes so she came up with an ingenious solution. She blacked her toes with soot from the stove and that helped hide the condition of her shoes.

Back then there was no welfare as we know it today. For desperate cases there was something called Relief also known as being "on the county". People had a lot of pride then and the ones that got relief were looked down on. I overheard the grownups talking about a man coming to the relief office asking for a sack of flour to feed his children. They gave it to him but sent someone to follow him to see if he was telling the truth. Looking in a window, he watched as the mother mixed flour and water together and gave it to the children to eat while she made biscuits.

Hal and Odie Smith had a little hardscrabble farm on the left hand fork of Cow Run. He worked as a hired hand for my Uncle Harve. With several children to feed and clothe, they had a hard time. Someone went to the Relief office and reported the Smiths needed help, so they sent a woman to investigate. Odie was so indignant that someone would think that they needed to be "on the county" that she took a broom and chased the woman off. Odie didn't have much but she had pride. Odie died young, worn out by hard work and little appreciation. Hal soon married again and started another family.

"Thresh" Machine a Comin'

That's what we kids hollered. You could hear it for miles, the "putt putt" of the big old Rumly tractor pulling the gigantic threshing machine. Everyone, young and old rushed to their front yard to watch as it slowly made its' way along the dusty road. We older children cheered and clapped our hands while the small children peered from behind their mother's skirts at the monster that was awfully big and awfully noisy. We young girls were excited about the threshing machine but we were particularly excited to see the driver. We all had a crush on him. He was so good- looking with dark curly hair and so different from the young boys around Cow Run. He was from "Mud Sock" and his name was Ross Gerlach. He proudly drove the big machine with his father, Earl Gerlach, standing behind him. I'm sure Ross, who was probably twelve or fourteen, must have got a kick out of everyone watching.

The pre-fall weather of August with its sometimes scorching days and steamy nights ushered in the threshing season. Most families raised wheat and had made arrangements for the threshing crew to visit their farms.

The housewives were in an unspoken competition with each other to fix the best meal. They were looking forward to showing off their culinary skills. They knew there was a lot of work in preparing to feed the threshing crew but the excitement was contagious. This was a change in the boredom of everyday living.

Not only did they want to prepare the best meal, they wanted to put all the foods they had available on the table. For instance, if there were six different kinds of pickles or jellies in the cellar, each would show up on the table.

The housewife would have fresh green beans from her garden, pickled beans from her cellar, a dish of brown beans, a dish of butter beans, a dish of Great Northern beans, all seasoned with plenty of side meat and to top them all off, baked beans oozing homemade catsup and molasses from their own sorghum patch. There were all kinds of vegetables, corn, peas, and tomatoes fixed in various ways. I remember mashed potatoes piled high with a lump of butter on top, melting its way down; a sprinkle of black pepper enhanced the picture. The big platters of fried chicken had been cooked early that morning. Remember there was no refrigeration; the chickens would have had to have been butchered the night before, put in salt water in a big kettle, covered tightly and set on the cellar floor until early morning when it was fried. Two or three kinds of cakes and several varieties of pies made choices for desserts difficult.

Potato salad with plenty of sliced green onions and chopped hard boiled eggs boasted its own homemade boiled dressing which was also used on wilted lettuce, coleslaw and deviled eggs. These dishes were also on the table.

Every housewife made this boiled dressing. Nothing was measured, just stirred together and tasted until it seemed right.

Boiled Dressing

Beat 1 or 2 eggs; add 1 or 2 teaspoons of flour. Beat; add a dollop of apple cider vinegar, and a teaspoon or two of sugar. Add a sprinkle of salt. Now pour in some cream. Stir and taste. If it's not tart enough, add a little vinegar.

Not sweet enough? Stir in another spoonful of sugar. Cook over low heat, stirring constantly, until thickened.

Cooking was a lot of guesswork back then.

For the faint of heart, I've worked out a substitute recipe. I've been making this dressing for over sixty years by the "taste and guess method" so its time I got it down to real measurements.

Boiled Dressing

Beat 1 egg, add 2 teaspoons flour, 1 ½ tablespoons sugar, ¼ cup good apple cider vinegar, and ½ cup coffee cream, or "Half and Half" or evaporated milk. Add a tiny pinch of salt and beat. Cook over low heat, stirring constantly until thickened.

This makes enough for a dish of wilted lettuce. Pour it over the lettuce while the dressing is hot. For threshers you will need to quadruple the recipe or more!

Usually there would be at least two women working, getting all the food ready. To this day, we use old sayings like "You've fixed enough for threshers!" when we think someone has really gone all out on a meal. There was no shortage of volunteers to work with the threshing crew. They knew they were going to get a fabulous meal. Some farms had dinner bells. Some did not. Promptly at noon, one of the children was sent to the threshing set. The child felt very important when he announced "Dinners Ready."

The Rumly tractor and the threshing machine were immediately shut down and the men made their way to the house. A bench would have been set up in the back yard with a wash pan, a bucket of water, a towel and a bar of soap. There was much joking and teasing as the men washed up, each telling another to go ahead in and eat.

There were always two tables, sometimes three. One table full of men would eat and then go outside and sprawl on the ground under a shade tree and rest. The women would hurriedly refill platters and dishes for the next table. Earl Gerlach and his crew always ate at the first table. The men rested an hour from the time they shut down the machinery until they went back to work.

The best thing about getting threshing over with was that we would have fresh new bedding. We slept on straw ticks. They were sewn from blue and white striped ticking. There was a center seam with a neatly bound 24-inch center opening. We took our straw ticks, with the old straw in them, to the chicken house and emptied them. The chickens scratched and sang contentedly as they welcomed the new litter.

The ticks were then washed in the Maytag wringer washer and hung on the clothesline to dry in the sun. Next, they were spread out on the floor of the screen porch and stuffed with fresh new straw. When they were tightly filled, the center openings were safety pinned shut and the ticks were placed on the beds. These were our summer mattresses. In winter a feather tick was added on top of the straw tick. This made for a warm nest to snuggle into. It was frequently below freezing in our bedrooms.

Actually B.T. (before tractors) in the late 1800's, there was a threshing machine working in the Cow Run area. Run by brothers, Nick and Ben Hunt, with the help of Pete Sayre, it was powered by eight powerful draft horses. I'm afraid I don't know how the machine worked but I do know two of the horses' names from way back then! Kate and Doll were the leading team!

In the Gerlach machine, the wheat pouring from a spout on the left side of the threshing machine went into two wooden buckets that held one-half bushel each. While one bucket was being emptied into a heavy cotton mill sack, the other bucket was filling. They put four one-half bushel buckets of wheat in each sack totaling two bushels. Two men worked in a shallow box about four feet by six feet. The box caught the spilled wheat lost when sliding one bucket out and the other bucket in under the spout. There was a counting device that would tabulate each bucket as it was moved into position.

This total count was what they used to figure the amount owed to the threshing machine owner. The men in charge of filling the wheat sacks were older men usually not expected to do the harder jobs.

Earl Gerlach and his son, Ross, plus two other men made up his crew. Chester Kinzel was one of Earl's regular crew. The other workers were furnished by the farmer.

The old type threshing machine required three men to stack the straw and two men to cut the sheaves open and feed them into the machine.

Sometime in the mid 1930's, Earl traded his threshing machine in on a newer model. This machine, although not new, had many improvements. It had a blower, which could be controlled with levers to blow straw into a stack thus eliminating the three men usually needed to stack the straw. This blower blew the straw through a large pipe twelve or fourteen inches in diameter. The pipe could be telescoped in or out to place the straw exactly where they wanted it.

The newer machine also eliminated two men cutting the strings and feeding the sheaves into the big machine. They were replaced by a conveyor belt, which fed the knife device, which worked on an arm assembly that rotated to cut the string on each sheaf of wheat as it moved forward on a conveyor belt mechanism. There were several belts running between pulleys, none of which had safety covers. They seemed to be just waiting to grab someone's sleeve. The word was Caution! Caution! Caution! and I never knew of an accident.

The threshing machine vibrated so much that it was necessary when setting it up to thresh, to dig eight inch deep holes for each wheel to set in.

The huge Rumly tractor that powered the threshing machine was a 1929 model that had been purchased by Earl Gerlach in 1930 in Marietta, Ohio. He drove the tractor home to Mount Alto, around 100 miles, staying overnight at farmhouses on the way home.

The Rumly tractor ran on kerosene or unrefined crude oil. The exhaust noise was tremendous and under certain conditions, there were large smoke rings.

The big old Rumly tractor still exists today. It belongs to another Earl Gerlach now, the great grandson of the first Earl Gerlach who purchased it seventy-nine years ago.

Our Kitchen and Our Everyday Food

Double windows were on one side of our big square kitchen. The "safe", with glass doors above and wood doors below, for good dishes and linens, was also on that wall. The big Kalamazoo range had a large square of oilcloth tacked on the wall behind it and skillets, baking pans and various pots were hung there. The table and chairs were on the third wall and the walk-in pantry and kitchen cabinet were on the fourth wall. This cabinet contained a flour bin that held twenty-five pounds of flour and a large breadboard, on which to knead bread. There was a rectangular cast iron kitchen sink in one corner of the kitchen. Of course, there was no running water but we were grateful to have a drain so we didn't have to go outside to empty any pans of water. The sink held a wash pan, a bar of soap and a towel. When mealtime was called, everybody lined up and washed their hands before they sat down to eat.

A slop bucket sat beside the sink and we were told to save every morsel of uneaten food and put in this bucket. To this day, many years later, I feel guilty discarding an apple core, without throwing it to the birds. This bucket was emptied into the hog trough everyday. The dishwater was even saved in it.

We always had plenty to eat. Smoke cured pork every day was delicious but it got a bit boring day after day. There were always mom's soda biscuits with real cow butter and apple and blackberry jelly. Potatoes, fixed in different ways, were at every meal. I liked them all, but graveled potatoes were the best.

How to Gravel Potatoes

Take an ordinary kitchen fork and a small container and head for the potato patch. Insert the fork into the side of a hill of potatoes. Gently try to remove some dirt without disturbing the potato plant. You should uncover some little potatoes. Pick some if they are more than marble size. Pull the dirt up around the plant so the remaining potatoes can continue to grow. Repeat this on other hills until you get enough for a mess. Wash and gently scrape the skins from the little potatoes. Do Not Peel. Boil these in a little water with a little butter added. When tender, add a white sauce made with real country thick cream. Cook for two or three minutes to allow the flour in the white sauce to cook. Enjoy! Graveled potatoes are only possible when the potato patch is about half grown.

Another favorite was what we called "potatoes with their jackets on". Small potatoes were chosen from the potato bin. These were boiled until tender, drained, and then set on the back of the stove to dry. They were served with their jackets on; you just slipped the skins off and mashed them with butter, salt and pepper. Delicious!

There was always a large assortment of vegetables on the table in addition to potatoes. In the winter there was always some kind of dry beans as well as canned green beans, cooked with pork. There would be creamed corn, creamed tomatoes, etc. If a vegetable was creamed, it was dressed with a white sauce made with real country cream. In the summer, cottage cheese was homemade and so thick you could slice it. The slices would be drizzled with yellow cream and sprinkled with a tiny bit of black pepper.

Breakfast consisted of fried pork ham, shoulder or "side meat". We never said bacon. Then there was what is now called red eye gravy. We never heard it called that and we certainly never put coffee in it! There was oatmeal, always cooked in a double boiler, fried eggs and best of all, mom's big soda biscuits. Mom never used baking powder in her biscuits. She kept a small container of clabber milk on the back of the big range where it would stay warm. Using this milk and flour and salt, she added soda. The amount depending on how sour she thought the milk was. Once in a great while, she wouldn't put in enough soda and the biscuits were big and white and tasted similar to sour dough bread. I loved that kind the best but mom would complain her biscuits weren't quite right. There sure was a lot of guesswork in cooking back then.

On Saturday, we sometimes had buckwheat pancakes. Mom would stand at the kitchen range frying pancakes, trying to keep up with us eating them. We put little gobs of butter on them, and then hot brown sugar syrup, freshly made, was poured over them. The syrup melted down through the butter and they looked and tasted delicious.

One of our favorite suppers was mush and milk. Mom stood at the kitchen range slowly sifting meal through her fingers into a double boiler. This had to be done very slowly or you would have lumpy mush. The double boiler was used everyday to fix breakfast oats. It was also used in making boiled custard for our favorite dessert, Cake & Custard. Mom wore new white canvas gloves when stirring the mush. It popped viciously and you would have had some burns. It was years before I learned how to make mush without all that bother. I learned from directions on a box of store bought meal. You mix one cup of corn meal with one cup of cold water, then stir in three cups of boiling water, mix, and then cook over low heat, stirring frequently for twenty five or thirty minutes. We still enjoy a supper of corn meal mush and milk occasionally. If there is any left, it gets fried for breakfast.

Of course, we used homegrown corn meal. You took your own corn to the miller and he ground it into meal for you, keeping a portion, it was called a toll, for him. Our miller was Cleve Sayre who lived in the head of the holler on the left hand fork of Cow Run. I remember when they first came out with yellow corn. The claim was if you planted yellow corn the yield would be much larger. Our family wondered if the yellow corn meal would be as good as the white. They were told it would be; well, it was not. Daddy soon traded yellow corn for white after trying one batch of yellow corn meal mush and one iron skillet of yellow corn bread.

Mom was noted for making the best cornbread. There again, she used sour cream to make it. She never, ever, put flour in her cornbread. She would say, "If I want cake, I'll bake a cake."

Grandfather Cozart and the Potatoes

Potatoes were the staple food more than any other, even pork. Every family had a potato patch in addition to a large garden. They also had a truck patch, which was planted later than the garden, which was "put in" as soon as the ground could be worked. Sometimes a frost or late freeze got the early garden if you couldn't find enough items to cover up the young tender plants.

There is a true tale about my grandfather Cozart and potatoes. It seems he had a tenant farmer living on a farm he owned on the Kanawha River. Grandfather furnished

11

potatoes for the man to plant and they were each to get half of the resulting potato crop.

During the summer, Grandfather came by to see how the potatoes were doing. Well, they were not doing well at all. They were pitiful scrawny hills of potatoes so he dug up a plant to see what was wrong. He soon solved the mystery. The tenant and his family had eaten the potatoes and planted the potato peelings!

Remember, people were hungry and there was no welfare then and if they had children, who could blame them.

Citizens Telephone System

From the time that I can remember our community as well as the surrounding communities was connected through the Citizens Telephone party line system. Each family had a big oak telephone in their "sittin" room, the words, living room, were never used. Each family had their own ring. Ours was a short, two longs and a short. Mom resented the fact that we had such a long ring; our neighbor's was three shorts. A card with a list of names and their rings was attached to the telephone.

In addition to the local party line, you could ring central, which was a switchboard in Cottageville, and get connected to other places like Ripley. You had to pay a fee for this service. I believe it was ten cents.

It was considered just a fact of life that everyone listened in on everybody's conversations. Actually they thought it was a right that went with owning a telephone.

Times were hard, entertainment was scarce and the party line filled a void in peoples' lives. One time when I was too young to go to school I was playing by myself in the pasture field. A chicken hawk had killed one of our white Leghorns and Daddy had set a steel trap and covered it with white feathers hoping to catch the hawk. I trotted across the field and there were the white feathers covering the trap. Since some feathers had blown off, I picked them up and patted them into place. Then I heard a snap and felt pain. The trap had caught me instead of the hawk. I cried and cried and tried to pull loose but the trap was firmly attached to something. There was no way mom could hear me, I was too far from the house. I cried and cried and finally a neighbor who lived on the hill above us heard me and came and released me. Then she took me to our house to tell my mom.

Daddy was teaching school and I begged mom not to tell him. She didn't but when he got to school the next day all the students knew about it. The woman who rescued me had gone straight to her party line telephone and spread the news about the hawk that didn't get caught and the little girl who did.

There was one disadvantage of this telephone system. The wires on the outside of the house had to be unhooked when a thunderstorm threatened. There was danger if lightning struck nearby, of electricity running in on the wire and starting a fire.

Butchering

Thanksgiving Day was butchering day. Daddy taught at a local one room school and back then schools were closed two days a year, Thanksgiving and Christmas. So no matter what the weather, butchering had to be done then.

Every spring Daddy bought two, eight-week old O.I.C. pigs and fattened them on skim milk and ear corn until they weighed around two hundred pounds each. This kind of hog made a lot of lard, which was needed for cooking and baking throughout the year.

Asking around would usually find a neighbor with spring pigs for sale. If not, the weekly newspaper, *The Jackson Herald*, would be sure to have some listed.

A burlap bag or gunnysack as it was usually called was used to transport the pigs. The squealing pig was picked up by his hind legs and deposited in the bag, which was then tied. A ride in our Model T Ford brought the pigs to their final destination, our hog pen.

There was one job with the pigs we children had to do. Using a corn cutter, we cut armloads of weeds for them. Horseweeds and pigweeds were favorites but if it was green, most likely they would eat it. During the 1930's drought we had to go clear to the "crick" (Cow Run) to find weeds.

If one or both pigs were males, they had to be castrated which was soon done. This was important. We had neighbors who sometimes, butchered hogs that they had not got around to castrating and their house always bore the smell of cooking boar meat.

Early on the morning of butchering day two neighbors arrived, one carrying a 22 rifle to kill the hog. We were probably the only family in the area that didn't own a gun.

A big iron kettle of water was hung over a roaring fire. The hog was killed and put in a barrel set on an incline dug into the ground. Buckets of scalding water were poured over the hog. The hog was sloshed and turned until the bristles could be removed with sharpened, big butcher knives. I never heard of hog scrapers back then. Next a gambrel stick was inserted through the tendons of the back legs and the hog was hung suspended from a tree or a temporary frame they had made for that purpose. The head was severed and put in a container of water to soak out the blood. A washtub was placed under the hog to catch the intestines. The best lard called "leaf lard" was that made from the lacy fat covering them.

The bladder was detached and given to the kids as a plaything. Using a hollow weed as a mouthpiece, it was blown up like a balloon and made a nice play toy.

The liver and melt were cut out and sent to the house to be cooked for dinner. They were cut into serving size strips, soaked in water for a few minutes, floured, and lightly browned in meat grease in iron skillets. A little water was added, the skillets covered, and placed on the back of the range and cooked slowly until it was mouth watering tender.

We always had a big dinner on butchering day. The fresh liver tasted so good, especially since we hadn't had any since Thanksgiving Day last year.

The hams, shoulders and side meat were trimmed well and placed skin down on the big meat table in the smoke house. Then they were covered generously with coarse salt.

Some people liked to pickle side meat and it was so good. Here are the directions given to me many years ago by a good neighbor and good cook.

Phyllis Hunt's Pickled Side Meat

Choose a stone jar the right size to hold the meat you want to pickle. After butchering, cool meat overnight until all animal heat is gone. Cut side meat into eight-inch squares or just cut a side into four pieces. Pack meat into jar tightly. Take cold well water and stir coarse salt into the water until it will float a fresh egg. Pour salt water over meat until jar is full. Cover with a cloth and weigh down with a plate topped with a river rock. Skim off scum and rinse out cloth when needed. Meat should be ready to use in about three weeks. Soak overnight, drain, roll meat slices in flour and fry slowly.

The tenderloin was cut from the backbone and sliced into pieces ready to pack into pint jars and can.

Mom would take a Mothers Oat Box, fill it with backbone and spare ribs, wrap it securely with brown paper and string and give to our mailman, Tuncil Wright, who would take it to the Cottageville Post Office. It would be put in the mailbag for Charleston, put aboard a train and grandma's Charleston mailman would give the meat package to her the next morning.

The lard had to be rendered. The large container was covered tightly and left out all night so that the cold weather could chill it and make it easier to cut into inch size pieces.

The fat was put in the big iron kettle with a little water added to keep it from sticking. The kettle was placed over a low fire and the fat cooked slowly. It was stirred often and by evening the water had evaporated, the lard had cooked out and the "cracklins" had gone to the bottom. The lard was poured into lard cans and used all year for cooking and baking.

All the meat scraps and sometimes a shoulder were ground for sausage using a large meat grinder borrowed from the Oke Crum family.

Mild Sausage

20 pounds ground pork
1/2 cup pickling salt
6 tablespoons ground sage
3 tablespoons pepper

Mix thoroughly (use your hands) Form into cakes, fry them, pack into hot sterilized glass jars and seal with rubbers or rings and zinc lids. Turn jars upside down. Now they would pressure can this sausage.

The head was cleaned and the jowls cut off to be smoked. Then, using an ax, the head was chopped into two pieces and cooked until tender. The bones and fat were discarded and the meat was put through a food chopper, ready to make mincemeat.

Mince Meat

3 pounds lean pork, ground
5 pounds apples, pared and ground
2 pounds raisins
1 pound currants
3 cups brown sugar, packed
2 cups white sugar
1 pint apple cider vinegar
1 tablespoon each cloves, allspice and cinnamon
1 teaspoon salt.

Simmer together until liquid is reduced to desired consistency. You may add most any kind of fruit such as a quart of drained cherries or pears.

It was the custom to send your neighbors who had not butchered yet, a mess of fresh meat, probably some spare ribs and sausage.

Later, when the neighbors butchered, they would send you a mess of fresh meat always making sure that they sent you a little more than you sent them.

A Winter Day

The alarm clock goes off. It is very cold in the house, below freezing, for the water bucket sitting on the kitchen cabinet, has frozen over. Daddy comes downstairs and attacks the little coal fireplace with the poker. Hopefully, there is still fire alive at the center. At bedtime the night before the fire had been covered as usual with slack coal.

This was very fine pulverized coal, which accumulated around the big pieces of coal in our coal pile. The idea was to keep the fire alive but smothered so it wouldn't burn much coal. The last step was to shovel ashes from the hearth over it.

The bedrooms were always freezing cold so we heated flatirons in the ashes, wrapped them in wool rags and each person took one to slide between the icy sheet blankets, which we used in winter. In summer we slept between nice white feed sack sheets. Bed covers were patchwork quilts in the summer and wool comforters in the winter. In our white feed sack nightgowns, made very full, we could draw our legs up and huddle in the nightgown until the bed gradually warmed and we could straighten our legs out. We all had nightcaps made from white feed sack scraps.

One of the subjects we studied at our one room school was "Health". I remember it was a tan hardcover book, which we all believed. The "book" said we should sleep with our bedroom windows open, all year, so that is what we believed and what we did.

After the coal fire began burning well, we crawled out of our warm nests and hurriedly dressed in front of the fire.

After we got dressed and emptied the chamber pots, we added heavy everyday outdoor clothes and with milk bucket in hand, went to the barn. We had climbed into the haymow the night before and forked down hay for the night. We had gone to the corncrib and got ears of corn to put in the feed boxes for the horses. They munched away while we milked the cows. When I was eight years old I was given my own cow to milk. I named her Pet and it was my responsibility to milk her morning and evening. She only had three useable teats. Probably mastitis had infected the fourth quarter of her udder at some time. She gave good rich milk and was a nice gentle cow, which is more than I can say about Ruby, the cow that I milked when Pet was dry.

The date a cow was bred was marked on a calendar and eight weeks before the end of the gestation, a cow was turned dry. That is less and less milk was taken from her until she was literally dry and she had a rest period until her new calf was born. By that time she was ready to be milked again.

Ruby was sneaky. She would be as nice as could be for a while and when you didn't expect it, she would explode in a kicking fit. Most cows kicked up underneath, Ruby kicked out at the person milking her, so the milk bucket, the milk stool and me would go flying. Big bruises from her hooves would send me crying to the house. Ruby was the meanest cow we had but Star was dangerous when she had a calf. We always kept the calves shut in the barn. Morning and night the cows were let in for a time so the calf could suckle. Star would be grazing on the church hill, a half-mile away watching the barn where she knew her calf was. If she saw anyone going to the barn, she would come running off that hill bellowing like a bull. We were scared that someway she could somehow get to us. Eventually she would give up running around and around the barn and go back to grazing. Then we would sneak out the barn door and run for the house.

Star scared Daddy when he witnessed her chase some boys crossing the far end of our pasture field. They just laughed about it, but Daddy realized she was dangerous and got rid of her.

If we had much milk it was run through the Dee Laval separator. Heavy yellow cream came out the small spout and skim milk out the larger. This milk was fed to the hogs, no one would have thought of drinking it. The cream was collected in a five gallon can to be taken to the railroad station and shipped to Blue Valley Creamery in Fairmont, WV, who would mail us a small check depending on the weight of the cream.

Our gasoline motor Maytag washing machine was so difficult to start that Daddy invested in a 32-volt electric system for the whole house. He bought a Delco plant and the smokehouse was modified to fit it and its double row of large batteries. The house was wired with each room getting an overhead light fixture. The bulky Maytag gasoline motor was replaced with an electric model.

One feature of the new, electric system we particularly enjoyed consisted of an electric wire run from the back porch down over the hill to a light in what mom insisted we call the toilet. Most people just said privy. The light conveniently turned on and off at the porch and the toilet could be lit up which was good if you had to travel there after dark. Of course, each bed had a chamber pot tucked underneath, for bedtime use only.

My brother's best friend in our one room school, Antioch, got to go home and spend the night with us as a special treat. This was after we got the 32-volt electric system and Thort was fascinated. I don't think he had seen electricity before. He just couldn't believe the one bulb electric light in the outhouse.

Helen Gatchel Lester, a friend of mine since high school, remembers, in the 1930's visiting her aunt and uncle who lived just outside of Cottageville. They didn't have electric in that area yet but they had signed with a gas company who had drilled a gas well on their property and wonder of wonders, they had free gas and they installed a gas heater in their outhouse. It was a few years before electric came to the area but in the meantime, they were sitting pretty (pun intended). Helen says it was so nice and toasty warm in that outhouse.

Spring Time Gigging

When Cow Run hills came alive with blooming dogwood, it was time to check Cow Run riffles for suckers. Then it was time to go gigging. Gigging required a gig, a long pole with a three pronged spear-like point attached to the end, a gunny sack to put the fish (suckers) in and a bright light. Since it has been a while since I went gigging, I didn't remember what we used for light. My brother tells me he made a basket of baling wire with circles formed and vertical pieces of wire woven in and out, close enough that the 10 or 12 inch basket would hold the burning pieces of old tires. That was our source of bright light. Discarded tires were hard to find and if you saw one protruding from a trash pile, you were in luck. Four pieces of wire approximately thirty inches long were run up through the basket and secured to the end of a short pole. You carried the basket of burning tire pieces, which had been cut in pieces with an ax, with the pole against your stomach and your left arm and hand stretched out under the pole supporting it. Your right arm and hand held your gig, ready to strike. We wore old cut off jeans and our worst tennis shoes. We always got wet all over but it was fun.

Riffles were shallow water flowing over gravel between deeper holes of water. We waded along until we came to a hole of water too deep to wade through. Then we had to get out on the creek bank and walk around that deep hole. Somebody had to carry a gunny sack to put the fish in and another sack containing the old tire pieces to replenish the burning basket as needed. The fish sometimes quickly darted away and quite often I missed it. It was great fun to see if I could strike quickly enough and accurately enough to land a fish. All the time I was thinking how good the fish were going to taste. I had learned that the quicker a fish was caught, cleaned, rolled in cornmeal and fried in "meat grease", the better it tasted. Suckers were not the best fish but "Hey, they were better than no fish at all." The creeks had been fished out and there were no lakes or ponds back then.

There have always been mischievous boys and Cow Run boasted their share, only Cow Run people didn't use the work mischievous; the word they used was ornery!

People were always laughing at any new pranks the boys thought up. Now this joke had to do with gigging.

Starling Hunt, one of the boys known for creating jokes had spent the early spring evening around the hill at Hode Shinns' and was on his way home using the path that encircled the hill above Cow Run. He saw lights and some people in the creek and realized they were gigging fish. At this time in the 1930's, gigging fish was against the law. Starling quickly realized it would be a good joke to make them think he was the game warden. He hollered, "Boys, I've got you now!" The people in the creek took off running in all different directions, their gum boots just a thumping the ground with Starling laughing so hard he was having trouble hollering, making like he was the game warden. Laben McClure and Bige Hughes, older men had been in the bunch that had been fooled. The next day when Bige found out the joke he said, "Someone ought to knock that _____ fool in the head."

The Kalamazoo Stove

About 1930 our family made a big purchase when they ordered a new cook stove. Every year we got a catalogue in the mail from the Kalamazoo Stove Company in Kalamazoo Michigan. Its glossy pages with all the big beautiful ranges pictured made it a wish book. Shipped by rail the stove was unloaded at the Cottageville train station. The yellow painted depot with its platform for loading and unloading freight stood beside the railroad tracks just south of where 331 comes into town from the West.

When, Mr. Bishop, the station master called on the party line to tell us we had freight, daddy hurriedly hitched up the horses and wagon and drove the three miles to Cottageville to get the stove.

The old black cook stove was carried to an out building and the new range put in its place. I was seven and in awe of the big black and white monster. It had two warming ovens and a reservoir for a constant supply of warm water if you kept it filled from the well.

With the stove there was a large black baking pan that just fit into the oven. Six large loaves of bread could be baked at one time. Making several loaves at one time makes it easy to tell when the bread is done. Just pull two loaves apart and check the middle.

I wanted to bake something in the new stove. I could read some and I looked at a cookbook, picking out and asking what the words were that I didn't know. I chose a recipe and learned to use the eggbeater and how to measure and stir the ingredients. Finally I had my first baking effort in the oven of the Kalamazoo stove.

Over the years cooking and baking has always been my passion. I have tried thousands of recipes, many of them my own, but none do I remember as well as that little seven year old girl, standing on a chair mixing her first recipe. I had chosen CORN MUFFINS and they turned out well, all golden and delicious, but I was so disappointed. Mom sometimes baked cake batter in muffin pans and I thought my muffins would be like hers, a sweet dessert. Instead I had made corn bread.

Saturday Night was Bath Time

Saturday night was bath time. No, we did not bring a washtub into the kitchen, like they show on old movies. We took a large wash pan and poured in steaming hot water from the teakettle, which always set on the big cook stove. We added cold water from the bucket of drinking water which always set on the kitchen cabinet .We got a wash cloth and a bar of soap and set the pan on a kitchen chair in front of the fireplace. We locked the door and stripped off the clothes we had worn since the Saturday before. We used to laugh and say wash down as far as possible, wash up as far as possible, and then wash possible. I had a bit of trouble with my long underwear. The cuff at the ankle stretched and I had to fold the excess over and try to work the heavy stockings up over the resulting bulge. Then they had to be pulled up over the knees and held with round elastic garters. I still remember how good it felt to take that sponge bath and put on fresh clean clothes.

Sayre Reunion

There were a lot of Sayres so the reunion was at the Evans fairground under the big oaks next to the Otterbien Church. The adults visited relatives they hadn't seen since the year before and we children became reacquainted as we played happily together.

Dinner was spread on second best white damask tablecloths right on the grass. There were no picnic tables or chairs. Everyday china plates were used. The silverware had colorful string bows on the handles so everyone could find their own.

Some people spread patchwork quilts to sit on.

Everyone wore good clothes to picnics. The men wore their Sunday suits, the women and children their best clothes. I always got so dirty playing. Mom washed my face and hands at the well and put a clean dress on me for afternoon.

Most people brought about the same food, of course there was no refrigeration and chicken had to be fried that morning. The potato salad and deviled eggs, both made with delicious homemade mayonnaise were finished. Mom's famous banana white cake and her apple sauce pies along with pickles, jelly and store bought bread were added.

The food was not packed away after we ate, it was covered with a tablecloth and left so anyone that got hungry could help themselves.

For special occasions, like the annual Sunday school picnics, the Sayre reunion or granddad's birthday picnic, mom made a special cake, a cake that she was noted for. She used the Lady Baltimore white cake recipe from the old Rumford baking powder cookbook from 1908. For our everyday cakes she used our own country butter but for this cake she sent to the store and bought Crisco.

Ella Sayre's Special Cake

¾ cup fine granulated sugar
½ cup butter (she used Crisco)
½ cup milk
1 ½ cups cake flour
1 level teaspoon Rumford baking powder
3 egg whites
1 teaspoon pure vanilla

Beat the butter or Crisco with the sugar until very light and creamy. Put the vanilla in the milk and add alternately with the flour and baking powder, which have been sifted together. Beat the egg whites until stiff and fold into the creamed mixture. Grease two 8-inch cake pans and dust with flour. Bake in medium hot oven twenty minutes or until broom straw inserted in middle of pan comes out clean.

Now what made this cake special is what she did next. She had sent to the store for two or three nice ripe bananas. She sliced them lengthwise in one-fourth inch thick slices and curved them to completely cover the top of one of the cake layers. This would be the bottom layer. Next she made the frosting.

Boiled Frosting

1 cup granulated sugar
1/3 cup hot water
1 egg white
1/6 teaspoon cream of tartar
1 teaspoon vanilla

Boil the sugar and water together without stirring until it forms a thread when a spoonful is lifted from the pan. Pour the hot syrup over the egg white, which has been beat stiff with the cream of tartar. Add vanilla and beat until thick enough to spread. Pour some on the bananas then place other layer on top and frost the cake.

Then the cake was placed in a large pan covered tightly and set on the cellar floor. By the next day, the banana flavor had permeated the cake and it brought rave reviews.

Picnics

There were three picnics to look forward to each summer. The Sayre reunion, granddad's birthday picnic, granddad being George W. Sayre, affectionately known to everyone as "Pap" George and the third was the annual Antioch Sunday school picnic. This was another great day for the community to get together. The attendance was always larger than usual on picnic Sunday. For the children, it was so exciting to see where we would go from year to year.

Loaded into a big cattle truck, we stood holding onto the side racks, leaning one way or the other as we sped around curves. Of course, a few older people traveled by car.

One year we visited our magnificent new state capitol in Charleston, WV. Most of our crowd had not been there. So after we spread our picnic on the grounds and we ate our fill, we toured the capitol, seeing both the Senate and House of Representative chambers. We were awestruck at the high crystal chandeliers especially the one in the rotunda.

The designation I liked best of all Sunday school picnics was when they loaded everybody on the ferryboat and took us from Letart part way across the Ohio river to Letart Island. They left us there and came back in late afternoon to pick us up.

We picnicked under the trees and explored the white sand beach. In the shallows, the water was crystal clear and only eight or ten inches deep. I always loved the water so I went wading and got yelled at!

Our Snacks

Every household raised some popcorn. We shelled it as we popped it. The ears were only four to six inches long and the easiest way to shell it was to rub two ears together over a pan to catch the kernels. Then about a third of a cup was put in the popper basket. This had a long handle which allowed us to hold it over hot coals without getting too hot ourselves. Never, ever did we hold it over an open flame. To do so would be a disaster. The popcorn in the basket would erupt in flames and we would have the problem of what to do with the resulting charred mess. Most didn't add a sprinkle of salt and we never heard of using butter, it was so good just the way it was.

Most farmers raised a patch of cane so they could have a supply of sorghum molasses for the winter. This was their "sweetening". Sugar from the store was too expensive.

One of the fun things we did back in the 1930's was to all get together on a Saturday night at someone's home and pop popcorn and make popcorn balls. These directions come from Evelyn Riffle who still makes popcorn balls the way her mother did in the 1940's.

Popcorn Balls

Pop popcorn, discarding any bad kernels.
Heat one cup of molasses to boiling for two minutes. Be careful, it scorches easily. Add a teaspoon of soda. Stir. Cook one minute and pour over popcorn. Butter your hands and shape into balls as it cools.

Apples from the cellar and hickory nuts and black walnuts were welcome snacks. Black walnuts were gathered, hulled, dried and taken to the railroad station in Ripley where there was a collection point with scales. Selling the walnuts brought a little cash money. The rate was usually $1 a hundred pound, but during the 1940's, we got $4 a hundred pound and we thought we were rich! During the 1930's, my dad would sometimes parch corn in an iron skillet. That was an old pioneer snack. Indian scouts like Jesse Hughes who traveled this area on the lookout for savages didn't have time to stop and fix something to eat. They depended on their little bag of parched corn to keep them going.

If we got a nice fluffy snowfall, we could count on snow cream. This was so good. With no electric and no refrigeration, we seldom got a taste of ice cream. This is how we made it.

Snow Cream

1 egg
½ cup heavy cream
1 teaspoon vanilla
3-4 tablespoons sugar or to taste
tiny sprinkle of salt
Beat egg well. Add other ingredients, beat. Stir in light fluffy snow, with a spoon until mixture is stiff. Eat quickly.

My father thought playing cards was evil and would have had a stroke if anyone had dared to bring a deck of cards into our house. To this day, I do not know the names of the playing cards.

My aunt visited us and brought us two games, Flinch and Touring. It took some persuading but Dad was finally convinced that these games wouldn't corrupt us! I quickly became quite popular since no one else had card games. Everyone craved entertainment and we spent many winter evenings sitting around some family's big kitchen table playing Flinch and Touring. We young folks sometimes got together for an impromptu party at somebody's home and made candy. This was usually tied to a music party. We were fortunate to have several musicians on Cow Run, most of them from the Nancy and Hode Shinn family. Their several children played several instruments. When one child finished playing and lay down an instrument, one of the others picked it up and started playing. They gave me an inferiority complex! Ray Hartley accompanied them with the French Harp. Edward would second on his guitar. Roger Pinnell would come; he was learning to play the French Harp. Luther Ohse would be there with his violin. He was really good. Everybody liked Luther. Sadly, he was killed at the Battle of the Bulge in World War II. Luther's father had come to America with the violin when he was only six years old. He was a very old man and I was a very little girl when I was fortunate to hear him play.

I've always remembered. He could make a violin talk. That violin is still in the family. When we had a music party those of us who didn't play instruments sang. I don't know how good we were, but we were loud. I remember being hoarse the next day after the music party.

One of those parties was at Hannah Hunt's and her son Roy's.

Every kitchen had a bench with a wash pan sitting on it. Everyone would wash their hands and I do mean everyone before every meal, whether you were at home or a visitor in someone else's home.

I remember this music party because of something that happened there that I am just now telling for the first time after all these years. I was probably about ten. Some of us had taken sugar and milk and we were making candy in the kitchen while others were playing music in the sitting room. I always wanted to be the "biggest duck in the puddle" and I insisted that I could take care of beating the chocolate fudge as it cooled. In order to cool it faster, the hot fudge pan was set in the wash pan, which, of course, contained dirty water from people washing their hands. While I was beating the fudge, the pan tipped sideways and a little dirty water slopped into the pan of fudge. I was horrified. I looked around, nobody had noticed. I didn't know what to do. I just kept beating, knowing all the while that a little dirty water was being incorporated into the fudge. I said nothing and everybody seemed to enjoy the chocolate fudge. Here is the recipe we used for chocolate fudge. It was first published in a cookbook in 1908.

Chocolate Fudge

2 cups sugar	1 teaspoon vanilla
1 cup milk	
6 tablespoons cocoa	
1 tablespoon butter	

Cook sugar, cocoa and milk together until a little dropped in coldwater forms a very soft ball. Remove from fire and add butter and vanilla. Beat until mixture thickens. Pour into buttered pan and cut into squares.

Notice there is no chocolate chips, no marshmallow cream and no confectioner's sugar
This is real fudge.

Owl Hollow School

This story was told to me many years after it happened by two of the girls who lived it, Hazel Hughes and Olive Anderson.

Tucked away at the very head of Cow Run Valley, where the creek meanders to a trickle at its beginning, was a one-room school called Owl Hollow. Some students walked a path from Baden ridge, down over the big hill and through the woods to get to school. Other students came from nearby hollows.

Tuncil Wright was the teacher, and not only did he teach the eight grades of the school, the three "R's", readin', 'ritin', 'rithmetic, he also taught them about sports. He taught them basketball. None of them had ever seen a basketball game. Most of them had never even seen a basketball.

He had five girls, Hazel Hughes, Olive Anderson, Grace Hartley, Freda Wedge and Daisy Barr who learned the game well, so well in fact that the teacher decided to challenge Cottageville School to a girl's basketball game. Cottageville School was over four times as large as the little one room Owl Hollow School.

Justine Wright, the teacher's sister made uniforms for the girls. They practiced diligently but a few days before the game, tragedy struck. Daisy Barr's mother refused to let her take part in the game because she would have to ride in a car the six miles between the two schools and the car might wreck and she might be killed! Cars were a fairly new invention, there were few in the county and some people were afraid of them.

Hazel and Olive walked several miles to Daisy's home to try to persuade her mother to let Daisy go to Cottageville and take part in the basketball game. She refused. Since Daisy was such a good player, they didn't know how they could play without her. Someone, probably Justine, came up with an ingenious solution to the problem. John Kerwood was one of the smaller boys in the school. In fact he was about the same size as the girls on the team and he was good at basketball. So the answer was to put John Kerwood in Daisy Barr's uniform and have him play in her place. Justine hastily made caps for each of them so the girls could tuck their hair up out of sight and not look too different from John who of course had a boy's haircut.

Eighty years have since wiped away the memory of the exact score, but Owl Hollow School beat the Cottageville School and some were heard to say that they could not believe how high that Daisy Barr could jump!

Granddad G.W. Sayre Birthday

Screams from the backyard, where children were playing, interrupted granddad's birthday picnic at our house one summer in the late 1920's. One of granddads great grandchildren, Bill Pinnell, had managed to get the lawn mower out and was pushing it around through the group of children when he cut off the end of Kathleen Meredith's finger. Her grandmother, Arkie Sayre, grabbed a tin cup, poured kerosene, which everyone called lamp oil, in it and stuck the little girls hand in it. Kathleen, also a great grandchild, had a stub finger for life and mom said she never could stand to use that cup after that. When Grand-dad got older, he had retired from farming on Cow Run and bought a big house on the main street in Cottageville. He had seven acres, which bordered on Mill Creek behind the house. He kept a milk cow, a flock of chickens, several hives of honeybees and raised a garden. Eventually the birthday dinners were held there. Granddad always had a mutton butchered for the occasion. I never liked it but when I got older, I realized it was the way they cooked it. They boiled it! When we raised sheep, I learned to roast it. There is no other meat as tasty as roast lamb or brown gravy as good.

Roast Lamb

Using a sharp knife, trim all fat and membrane from the meat and discard. Place lamb in an open pan, sprinkle with a little salt and pepper and roast at 325 degrees until done. Remove to a heated platter while you brown bits. Discard the fat. Add flour to the pan and cook over low heat stirring constantly. Then slowly, add a small amount of water. Cook three or four minutes until it looks like the best gravy you've ever tasted.

Chicken was about the only meat used at these dinners. Cured pork would have been available but we ate pork every single day for breakfast, dinner and supper and we looked forward to something different. Young chickens, fryers were usually only raised in the spring so an old hen or rooster was usually used. Mom simmered the chicken pieces until they were done then dipped them in batter and fried them. If the chicken being prepared was a hen rather than a rooster, there might be immature eggs inside. These were cooked with the simmering chicken and were so delicious. Women were always looking for a different way to fix chicken. One year, when I was a child, someone brought a different chicken dish to granddad's dinner. I can remember the discussion. Everyone wanted the directions and I have the original scrap of paper with mom's writing explaining how to turn a chicken into:

Smothered Chicken

Cook chicken until it leaves the bone. Put chicken through grinder. Save broth. Mix cracker crumbs or toasted bread crumbs with chicken in broth. Make little cakes and bake.

This became a popular dish at picnics.

One Room Schools

Brown, Silver Valley, Beech Grove, Owl Hollow, Lone Oak, Fairview, Red Mud and Antioch, these were the names of one room schools in our area. We went to Antioch, which meant walking a mile west into the winter wind sweeping down the valley. Sometimes we turned around and walked backwards a few steps just to catch our breath. Of course we had to walk through pasture fields. Even with our four buckle arctic overshoes, which every one wore, we would have got stuck in the deep red clay mud if we had walked in the road. We did well to pick our way gingerly across the road to get from pasture field to pasture field. Going through pastures and meadows necessitated crawling through or climbing over barbed wire fences.

The first year I went to school I walked with my dad through the fields to the school he was teaching, Silver Valley. That was a longer walk and meant climbing steps and walking a footbridge across Cow Run that the Board of Education had had built.

Really, I think going to Daddy's school was a mistake. He said he had to be harder on me than the other students to avoid them thinking I was teacher's pet! Some of the students were old enough to be seniors in high school.

Only there weren't any high schools. I remember the larger boys playing at recess, by wrestling and one boy. Orris Scarberry, got hurt and was crying. His shoulder was dislocated. As a six year old, I could not believe that a big boy, probably sixteen or seventeen was crying. My daddy put the boy's shoulder back in place. That was a lot of excitement for a little one-room school!

My daddy did not like loaf bread; we called it "light bread". He liked hot biscuits with each meal and took leftover biscuits in his dinner bucket. No one said lunch box. The term wasn't used. His biscuit usually contained ham with a second buttered biscuit ready for some apple butter or blackberry jelly, which was put in a little jar in the bucket. I liked to take a little jar of milk and a wedge of cornbread to crumble in it for my lunch. The other students thought this very odd.

We attended school from September to March. No matter how much snow, how hard it was raining, or how near zero the thermometer showed, we were expected to be there. If there was high water, we took to the hills and walked around it. The schoolhouse was always warm when we got there. The janitor, usually an older student, was paid ten cents a day to have a fire built and the floor swept. Garnet Hartley had the job for some years. If it was very cold outside the children gathered around the big potbelly stove, crying as their fingers and toes thawed. Every one-room school had a flagpole and another one of the duties of the janitor was to raise the flag each morning and put it away properly at the end of the school day.

The girls' outhouse was in a corner of the schoolyard, the boys' in another corner. They were three holers. There was no privacy and none was expected. You never went by yourself. You always asked somebody to accompany you. Often all three holes would be occupied. Of course there was a Sears and Roebuck or Montgomery Ward catalog handy. Most of us had never even seen toilet paper. We didn't know the trick Artist Taylor, a friend of mine used. She tells me she took a page from the catalog crumbled it up and smoothed it out *three times.* Then it was much softer. Now, if we visited parents' outhouses, in addition to the catalogs there would have been a box of corncobs, which some adults used. Popcorn cobs were considered the best because they were softer than regular corncobs.

The outhouse was a good place for sharing secrets. I remember a discussion as to where babies came from. No one had any idea but one of the eighth grade girls said her cousin got fat before she got a baby. Interesting, but we could see no connection!

Most of the school year, the teacher boarded at a nearby farmhouse. The school bell rang at nine o'clock and school let out at four o'clock. Schools had anywhere from sixteen to thirty students with first through eighth grades. Two students sat side by side at double desks. Each desk had a bench on the front that made the seat for the next desk. In the front of the room was the teacher's desk and recitation bench, which was about ten feet long. For instance the teacher would ring a small bell and call fourth grade reading and the fourth grade students would take their reading books and go sit on the recitation bench. There they took turns reading aloud with the teacher helping with new words. On the wall behind the teacher's desk was a large blackboard. Right above it was the A B C s in both capital and small letters. Once a week we had a class in penmanship and tried to make our writing look like that. In the corner hanging on the wall was the library, which consisted of a small bookcase with some books, which I read over and over. There were two or three books by Gene Stratten Porter. There was *Pollyanna* and one year the teacher used pie supper money to order Victor Hugo's *The Hunchback of Notre Dame.* I tried to read it but fortunately it was over my head. There were some shabby wall maps, which pulled down like a window shade. Nails in the wall beside the door held coats and muddy overshoes were on the floor beneath the coats. The water bucket bench was there too with an open bucket and a dipper. The older students carried water from the nearest farmhouse. There was much competition as to which two were going to get out of school to go after water. Some schools, like Silver Valley and Brown had cisterns with a hand pump but at Red Mud the students had to go down the road to a spring and dip a bucket of water. You were never supposed to drink from the dipper so if you didn't have a tin cup from home you folded a sheet of notebook paper to make a cup.

There was a one-hour break at noon and a fifteen-minute recess in midmorning and afternoon. So we got a lot of playing done in that time. The school had a volleyball set, which had been ordered some years before with pie supper money. Sometimes we played with that, picking players until all were chosen even the ones like me who weren't very good. It really didn't matter, the taller players always hit the ball back over the net before we younger ones could touch it. We sometimes divided into two teams, one stationed on each side of the schoolhouse and played a game we called "Andy-Over". A pasture field across the road served as a baseball diamond and if we could find a ball we played there. "Boughtin" balls were hard to come by but usually someone had a homemade string ball.

There was a pretty little shallow creek called Grass Run that bordered our schoolyard and we often played there. We had fun building little dams in the creek. One time the bigger boys built a larger than usual dam across the creek and backed up the creek to a pond seven or eight feet wide and twelve or fifteen inches deep. Having completed that engineering job, they looked around for something else to do and decided to build a raft. Some broken pieces from a nearby rail fence together with some scraps of wood left from a cabin project they had once started were put together to form a makeshift raft. To our surprise, it floated! Sam Jones, one of the older boys, was standing balancing himself on the contraption in the middle of the little pond when the teacher, Kathleen Mann, walked across the schoolyard to see what was going on. She took one look and hollered, "Sam Jones, you get off there right now!" Sam immediately stepped off the raft into water up to his knees. The teacher sputtered, "I didn't mean for you to do that." Sam said, "Teacher, you said, right now."

We divided into two Indian tribes and called ourselves Cherokees and Delawares. We built a small fire and tried to cook something we had brought from home, often ending with a half raw potato. All boys carried pocketknives and sometimes we girls would borrow one to cut sticks with. No one got cut and no one got burnt. All children were taught from an early age not only to respect such things but how to use them.

Two older boys had homemade, heavy, wooden sleds that they brought to school when we had a snowfall. A big hill across the pasture field was just the spot for sled riding. We would spend the whole noon hour taking turns with four on the sleds. We shouted and laughed and had a wonderful time until one noon hour tragedy struck. The sleds coasted downhill just fine, but there was no way of steering. So when a sled hit a slight bump it threw it sideways just enough to take its" downward path to the side of the track they had been using and the sled crashed into a rail fence at the bottom of the hill. An older student, Charlotte Sayre was bruised and banged up some but a middle student, Starling Hunt suffered a broken leg. He was crying with pain lying there in the snow. Some students went to get the teacher. She sent the two oldest boys, Quentin Sayre and Edward Hartley, who were ice-skating nearby, to get Starling's parents, who just lived one farm away. Fortunately the muddy road was frozen so they were able to drive their Model T to the school and take

Starling to a doctor and have his leg set. That day our sled riding ended.

It was a cold winter's day with several inches of snow on the ground. Inside the one room schoolhouse was toasty warm. Someone had really fired up the big old Burnside pot bellied stove. One class was shuffling their way up to the recitation bench while another class returned to the seats. Someone shrieked, "Fire!" pointing to the area of the bead board ceiling surrounding the stovepipe. I don't know who had the bright idea, Lawrence Hunt was the teacher, but the students ran back and forth to the outside making and throwing snowballs at the fire until the flames were extinguished. If it hadn't been for the snowfall, Antioch School would have burned to the ground. That was over 60 years ago but the old school house still stands today. If you happen to be in the neighborhood, do drop by and stick your head in the door and look up at the stovepipe hole in the ceiling and you'll see the burnt area. Then think of the students who saved their school by throwing snowballs.

Kathleen Cunningham Mann was a well-liked teacher at Antioch. In the late 1930's as the school year ended, she had a big surprise for her students. She was going to take them to the movies. There was now a theatre in Ripley. She enlisted the help of one of her Cunningham brothers and they put straw and blankets in the back of a truck for the children to sit on and off we went on a nice Saturday afternoon. I had finished the eighth grade and wasn't actually one of her pupils but I got to go anyway. I don't remember how many we were, less than twenty I'm sure. Most of the young folks had never seen a movie. The smaller ones and some of the older students didn't understand that it wasn't real. I think the name of the movie was *The Trail of the Lonesome Pine*. I remember it was in color with beautiful mountain and lake scenery. There were very high train trestles and somehow a little boy was on a runaway locomotive which fell off a high bridge in a spectacular crash, of course killing the little boy. Most of us were teary eyed but the younger ones were really upset. I remember one little boy in particular, Waldo Sayre. He was really crying. He, like others, thought it was all real. I'm afraid their very first movie wasn't all fun for them.

Pie Suppers

The social event of the year for one-room schools was the annual pie supper. This was a necessary event for the money made paid for things for the school, such as a wooden box of chalk, some books for the library, perhaps even a volleyball set etc.

Since people came miles for these socials, the school had to be careful not to choose the same Saturday night as another school. Of course there was no electric. Two or three oil lamps in metal brackets on each sidewall made enough light. People sat at students' desks or stood around the walls. Most of the men stood around outside probably gossiping about the cattle auction they had attended that day or the coon hunt they had been on the night before. It was sometimes whispered that someone had brought moonshine.

Every unmarried female from seven to seventy could bring a pie to be auctioned, but actually it was the teenage girls who brought the majority of the pies. What girl brought what pie was supposed to be a secret but the boys watched carefully while pretending they were not watching! The pies were always cream pies butterscotch, vanilla, lemon, chocolate etc. I remember envying a luscious, lemon pie with mile high meringue which Ada Ruth Sayre brought. My butterscotch that I had thought was so pretty didn't even compare. Ray Hartley was the auctioneer and he tried to get more than twenty-five cents a pie, which was the usual price for pies at a pie social. Some boys got in a bidding war when each wanted to be the one to share a pie with a certain girl. When the bidding neared a dollar there was a stir from the crowd as everybody watched to see which boy would be fool enough to spend that much for a pie!

As each pie was auctioned, the high bidder was handed his pie and the girl who had made it joined him and they ate the pie together. Pie pans were only 8 inches then so the couple could usually finish the pie. Some cakes and some extra pies were auctioned to the crowd and then there was the cakewalk. An extra pretty cake was saved for this. Each couple paid five cents to walk for the cake. Couples lined up forming a circle and marched around until the judges called stop. The couple who was nearest to a predetermined mark when they stopped got the cake. They could keep it or they could do what most couples did, share it with the other couples.

At Christmas there was always a program with recitations, a play and a Christmas tree. This was in the afternoon of the day before Christmas. Each child in the school had a part in the festivities and their families came to see them perform. Teachers gave each child a brown paper bag containing their Christmas treat. Some teachers had the reputation of giving a better treat than others. My dad, John Sayre gave the best treat. He would buy hard candy, ribbon candy, stick candy, and chocolate drops, pour it into dishpans and give me the job of filling the bags. I enjoyed the job, counting out the pieces, making sure each bag had exactly the same amount and the same variety as the others. Last I dropped an orange and a banana into the bags. For the children this was a big deal, they seldom had candy and fruit. Another event the community looked forward to was "The Last Day of School". Families joined the children for a fun day of playing games and picnicking. Guests were mostly mothers and younger siblings, as fathers were busy with spring farm work.

Shivaree or Serenade

Around and around the house we marched, yelling, ringing cowbells, banging on pots and pans, with the occasional boom of a shotgun fired into the air. One time two men carried a large sawmill blade suspended from a pole through its center. When they hit that the sound was deafening. This celebration was called a shivaree in some areas of the country but in ours it was called a serenade. When a couple married the news spread quickly through the party line telephone system and a noise-making crowd soon gathered to interrupt their first night together. The noise continued until the blushing couple came out on the porch. The crowd began chanting "Treat, Treat" and the couple, who had known very well what was coming, was prepared with a treat for the crowd. Usually candy was passed around for the treat. When my brother, Clinton married Olive Anderson, they had gone to the melon fields down by the river and bought a load of watermelons so the crowd was treated to a watermelon feast.

When the Circus Came to Cottageville

In the early 1900's, the circus came to town, to Cottageville, actually. No, I don't remember it! This was before I was born. Frank Sayre who lived in Cottageville with his grandmother does remember it well.

This was an outstanding large circus with all matter of circus acts such as trapeze artists and brightly dressed circus wagons holding lions and tigers and many other animals not seen or even heard of by most of the crowds.

The circus traveled on the road from Ripley, they drove the animals into town on foot. A white stripe was put across all side roads and whether it was whitewash or chalk or even a strip of white cloth, the elephants wouldn't cross the white line. They had been trained to stay on the main road. The circus set up on the seven-acre bottom bordering the Mill Creek side of the village.

This must have been a most refreshing pause in the circus people's schedule. There were trees and grass and the sparkling clear creek. They had a chance to rest and catch up on laundry. There was a problem, however. This was before the construction of all the locks and dams on the Ohio, so the water level was much lower and the creek banks were straight up and down and high. There was no way to get the elephants down to water them. So they drove the elephants and water buffalo down the main street to what was well known as the "Deep Hole", below the Cottageville mill and dam. Of course, this delighted the townspeople. After all, how often do you see elephants on the street of a sleepy little town in West Virginia? The elephants enjoyed their bath so much; the handlers had a time trying to get them back to the circus grounds.

There have always been tall tales told about the Cottageville "deep hole". Usually they go like this. The road to Millwood curved sharply high above the water and a wagon, horses, driver and all got too close to the road edge and went over, straight into the "deep hole" where they just disappeared under the surface. Sometimes it's a horse and buggy and a couple that go under. I've even heard one version of a threshing machine disappearing under the water, never to be seen again.

It was a favorite swimming hole but most swimmers stayed near the edge. Repeatedly, adventurous swimmers have tried to reach the bottom, but to my knowledge, no one ever has. Several yeas ago, a young man, Mike Miller, an expert swimmer, drowned there.

The "deep hole" looks different now. The Racine locks on the Ohio River have raised the water level covering up the picturesque, cut stone dam as well as the "deep hole" where once many years ago elephants played.

Cottageville, Then and Now

Probably the first white man to set foot in the Mill Creek area was in 1797 when two hunters from the fort at Belleville came to the area to hunt deer. They were fired upon by Indians; one man named Coleman was killed and scalped, the other man, though wounded escaped. Coleman had a double crown and the Indians got credit for two scalps. Coleman was buried somewhere within the area of what is now Cottageville. The next year, 1798, one or two settlers actually settled in the area. These settlers pounded their corn into meal with a mortar and pestle to make bread. The next year, a Mr. Hushan brought a hand mill and erected it on the bank of Mill Creek. This place immediately took the name of Hushan's Mill. This hand mill operated until 1802 when a man named Benjamin Wright brought a horse powered mill and the location became Wrights Mill.

At this time, a post office was started called Cedar Grove. After a sawmill was built, a crude bridge was constructed across Mill Creek. Bridge piers were made up of logs in the form of a square as though they were building a chimney. Two piers were made, one on each side of the creek. Then two gigantic logs were laid across as sleepers. Finally, a floor of soft planks was pinned to the sleepers. This bridge was used until the fall of 1858 when a covered bridge called a wagon bridge was built, originally roofed with shingles. Later this bridge was roofed with galvanized iron. This covered bridge was used until the early 1920's when it was replaced by the present structure.

About the year 1845 or 1846, Wright sold his mill to a man named Moore and it became Moore's Mill. He built a crude dam across the creek and ran his little mill by water-power.

The valley continued to grow. It now had a prosperous woolen mill owned by a Mr. Roseberry. In 1858, Daniel

44

Rhodes came from New York; he purchased the mill, the store and the land. He also became postmaster. They got one, sometimes two, mail deliveries each week from the steamboats on the Ohio River. Mr. Rhodes thought the settlement had a bright future so he had it staked off in lots and streets, forming a town. Then he built a new large flouring mill. The products from here would be sold on many distant markets such as Philadelphia, New Orleans and Baltimore. Daniel built a two-story eighteen-room house with a large store constructed beside it. In order to supply waterpower for the huge mill, a massive stone dam was constructed reaching across Mill Creek. Five smaller homes called cottages were built for his family members. The area had now been known as Rhodes Mills but Daniel and his brother, George decided to call the town Cottage Mills from all the cottages being built. On February 24, 1860, Daniel changed the town name to Cottageville. Not long after that, the Civil War broke out and Daniel became a prisoner of war, accused of aiding the Union forces.

The town continued to grow. A shoe factory was started in 1872. It employed seven men and three women. The town could celebrate several firsts. They had the first post office, the first school, the first Sabbath school, the first tannery, the first bridge, the first mill site, etc. in the county.

In 1883 the town boasted four general stores, one drug store, one flouring mill, one hotel, one post office, one tannery, one harness shop, two blacksmiths, two resident physicians, one two-room school, two teachers and one minister.

Later a brick factory was started. At one time there was a bank, an undertaker, a theater and a hardware store. I can remember a milliner shop and getting my hair cut in one of the two barbershops. There was an ice cream shop too and I don't want to forget the yellow painted train depot.

From the time I can first remember him, my grandfather; Pap George Sayre had retired from active farming and lived in a two story yellow house on the main street in Cottageville. He was eighty when he left his Cow Run farm, but still kept abreast of farming decisions since he had his son, Harve, running the farm for him. Two other retirees from Cow Run joined him on Main Street, "Hen" Hartley and "Fish" Hunt. The tale was they all lived on the interest, which was three percent, on their money. A loaf of bread was 5 cents then, now it's $1.50 and interest is still three percent!

My grandfather and his second wife, Frances, owned seven acres along Mill Creek back of his house. They kept a cow from the farm for milk. They had chickens for eggs, they had beehives for honey and they raised a big garden.

Born in 1839, granddad, Pap George, lived to see Jackson County develop from a vast timberland wilderness to one of the richest of West Virginia's agricultural counties. Since he lived ninety-nine years, his life spanned an incredible culture change. He would sometimes tell his many grandchildren tales of his past. He told of going to Sayre School in the 1840's. There was a Sayre Church and a Sayre Cemetery too, built on land given by his father, David Sayre. One winter morning, when he got to their log school, he found their window gone. Their window was a greased paper over an opening created by cutting out half of a log. A hungry hound dog had eaten their window. School went on as usual with a cold west wind swirling through the opening. When he was older, granddad joined a crew rafting logs to New Orleans. At times, they would see Indians watching them from the shore. It was a very long way from Jackson County to New Orleans down the Ohio and then the Mississippi Rivers. It must have been scary for that was the only trip he ever made.

Now this is how he said Cow Run got its name.

In 1774, Colonel Andrew Lewis and an army of eleven hundred men traveled from Fort Union, now Lewisburg, to the meeting of the Ohio and Kanawha Rivers at what is now Point Pleasant. It was a fast moving march it took them nineteen days. They could not hunt game, so they drove some cattle with them to butcher to feed the army. Well at least one of the cows they were driving escaped the butcher's knife and stayed in that area. Occasionally, someone would get a glimpse of the cow so they started calling the area Cow Run, even many years later and the name stuck.

Several years before his death, at the age of ninety-nine, Granddad had his coffin made by a grandson, Hoyt Crum who was a fine carpenter. It was as beautiful as a fine piece of furniture but it was lined with cheesecloth. My mother, Ella Cozart Sayre, took one look and ordered satin lining from a casket company. Then she sewed and quilted and padded until the interior duplicated that of a purchased casket. When he inspected the final results, Pap George said "Gawsh, Gawsh, that's fine enough to sleep in!"

Angerona

We frequently went to Add Sayre's big store at Angerona. I can find nobody who knows where the name Angerona originated. The town had been laid out by Nathan Ong in 1847 in what they said was the best section of the valley. It was a picturesque, little village nestled at the foot of an enormous hill called, what else, Angerona Hill. Mill Creek rushed by on one side, the site of a saw and gristmill. In 1883, Angerona had two stores, one tannery, a blacksmith shop and a post office. Five years later, a railroad was built and a train made daily runs through the little town on its way to Evans and Ripley.

I remember a big store, a big house, and a big mill. The house was yellow with white gingerbread trim. There was a concrete walk connecting the house and store, centered with a cistern and hand pump. My mom always said that Mr. Sayre, (she was probably the only one who called him Mr.), had the best dry goods and insisted that my brown leather high top shoes had to be Star brand and must come from Add's store. She would not buy at any of the stores in Ripley. She considered their goods inferior.

January 4, 1940 was a disastrous day for the town. Mr. Sayre had got up and built a fire, then went back to bed until the house warmed up. He fell asleep and was awakened by the sound of breaking glass and dense smoke. He and his wife escaped out an upstairs window. Since the house and store were only a few feet apart, the store was doomed. Mr. Sayre had stopped the milling business and turned the mill into a giant chicken house and went into the chicken and egg business. He had taken Daddy on a tour and I had tagged along, up narrow stairs, with rooms and rooms of white Leghorn chickens.

Of course, the mill burned too. It was just across the road. That was the end of Angerona. For a long while, the big railroad sign with Angerona on it stood tall but now it is gone and so too is the railroad. At least the road cutting through the remains of the town and snaking crookedly over the giant hill is officially on the maps as "Angerona Road."

Mud Sock or Mt. Alto?

Mud Sock was the name of a nearby town when I was growing up. I certainly had no idea that Mud Sock and a town called Mt. Alto were one and the same. This village was only about three or four miles from where we lived if you cut through the country on mud roads and went in the back way. I was a teenager before I realized that Mud Sock was a commonly used name for Mt. Alto. It was the newest town in Jackson County, having been laid out in 1871 by Thomas Turner. 1932 brought big news for the town. They became the "baby" of Jackson County's U.S. Post Offices. At long last, they had a U.S. Post Office of their own.

Mt. Alto was known as Mud Sock by everyone, except for the people living in the town and some of them used the more familiar name. In 1883, the town had one general store, one blacksmith shop, one cooper shop, one tannery, one school, one church and one doctor, Dr. A. Herrenkoh. Dr Herrenkoh came to Mud Sock in 1892 and spent his life with the townspeople and the surrounding community, doctoring their ailments and delivering their babies.

Later a large flouring mill was added. It served the southern part of Jackson County and bordering Mason County. Three more stores, an undertaker, and a hat factory brought more prosperity. On the north end of the one street town, a large two-story building held the undertaker's establishment on the first floor and the second floor was devoted to the hat factory. That's where two ladies designed and made hats. Now understand, that was a big business at that time. No self-respecting lady would have stepped gracefully up into her buggy without a charming hat on her head. There, in her wardrobe were hats for church, hats for market, elaborate hats for special occasions and even everyday hats.

After World War I, there were lots of rumors about German sympathies. The people's name that owned the flouring mill was Swartz. Somebody started a ridiculous rumor that they were putting crushed glass in the flour they made. Anyway, the big flouring mill burned. Rumors did fly then. It was whispered that the mill was torched because the owners were Germans. Who knows?

This is a tale that they say happened in the town. There was this old man who lived on a high ridge on the right hand fork of Cow Run. His wife died. Two or three days after the funeral, he made his way to Mud Sock and was asking people as to where he could find a woman or another wife. Someone said, "Why, Mr. Kemenah, your wife just died, you can't be looking for another so soon"! He indignantly replied, "Why she's just as dead now as she'll ever be!"

The Poor Farm

In the 1840's, the Jackson County Court appointed Commissioners to purchase land and build an infirmary. This resulted in the purchase of land on a country road near Cottageville and the construction of a 37-room clapboard house. The building was divided into two parts, one for the superintendent's family, the other for the inmates, who numbered between 20 and 40 at one time. The front yard was divided by a line fence as well.

You would expect the "poor house" residents to be old and feeble but such was not always the case. In the 1880 census, there were fourteen residents listed by names and ages, five of these were teenagers.

This was often the first stop for unwanted children who were meant to go to the Children's Home in Charleston as soon as they had room and that often took awhile. The mentally ill were often dumped here until a more appropriate place could be found, which could take months.

The payment for the position of superintendent was $50 per month. Apparently it was a political appointment.

Amos Wilkinson was the superintendent of the infirmary for 20 years from 1900-1920.

This was a productive fertile farm of 160 acres. They raised corn, wheat, oats and cane for sorghum as well as all kinds of vegetables. The superintendent with two hired hands and the help of any able-bodied inmate did the farm work. They were expected to be self-sufficient.

His wife supervised all those under the roof of the huge house. With the help of those inmates able to work, they worked without running water, bathrooms or electricity. Coal and wood were their fuel and it was reported that the huge building was terribly cold in winter and terribly hot in summer. Well, I think I know why. I remember when I was little, neighbors of ours from Cow Run, Charley and Martha Mullinex had gotten the appointment to run the place and we went to visit them on a Sunday afternoon. Of course, Charley took daddy on a tour of the "poor house" and, of course, I tagged along. I remember climbing bare wooden stairs to big rooms with bare floors and bare wood walls. The walls had gaps between the boards and you could see daylight. I may have been little but I thought how could people live there. It wasn't as good as a barn.

There were very few inmates there then. Eventually there were none and the county rented the farm to various tenant farmers over the years. Then the huge bare building stood empty until the early 1960's when somebody torched it. The resulting conflagration rained ashes on the countryside for miles around.

There is a home situated on a hill across Mill Creek, which overlooks "the poor farm". On this fateful day, the owner sat on his front porch and watched as a small plane landed in the field below the poor house. Some people climbed out of the plane and walked up to the house. They stayed a short time and then walked back to the plane and flew away. A little later, the big historic home called the "Poor Farm" was in flames.

In 1971, the Jackson County "Poor Farm" became the new site of the Jackson County Junior Fair.

So every year the last week of July finds a frantic hustle and bustle as a steady line of vehicles loaded with prize livestock turn into the gate and drive to their respective barns to unload.

The carnival midway is almost ready as the roustabouts set up one ride after another. Their food stands are already open. The smells of cotton candy, popcorn, hot dogs, funnel cakes, fried fish and curly fries blend together and spell "fair time".

The crowd grows larger but probably not one person thinks back to the time when these acres were the site of a thirty seven room house, the home of unfortunate humans who had no choice in how they lived the last of their lives.

An itinerant preacher would come with a sermon on most Sundays. He presided over the burials of those whose bodies were not claimed by a relative. Pine boxes were made to bury those who were placed in the "Poor Farm" cemetery. This is the cedar crowned knoll behind the present day amphitheater stage.

When Eugene McClure was a boy, he and his family lived in the seven-room superintendent's portion of the big house and farmed the land for the County Court. This was long after the inmates were gone.

He said that he and his dad, Laben cleaned and mowed the long neglected graveyard. There were only two or three graves with any identification.

I wonder if unseen ghosts of the past hover over the many unmarked graves among the cedars, only a few feet from the stage and the entertainers.

Old Time Religion

"Give me that Old Time Religion, it's good enough for me", that is how the song went and it was sung by the congregation at nearly every prayer meeting.

The vast majority of Cow Run people were religious. That is, they went to Sunday school at ten o'clock on

Sunday morning and most stayed for "preachin" on the two Sundays a month the preacher visited. Then there was always Wednesday night prayer meeting and a week or more of Revival or, Protracted meeting as it was also called, in late fall. By then, people had most of their fall farm work done.

An older man, Charley Mullinex, had no children to help him in his farm work so he was probably tired out for he always dozed off during meetings, his white head sinking down farther and farther, his bald spot shining in the rays from the Aladdin lamp. I was little, about six, and watched him wondering how he could sleep with the preacher hollering. The preacher always preached hell and damnation. It was scary and he meant it to be scary.

I remember vividly our next farm neighbors were clearing land and at night they burned huge brush piles on a high ridge, the orange flames reaching high into the black night sky. I was little and so scared. I thought that was like the hell the preacher was always hollering about.

Located near the head of Cow Run Valley, the earliest church in the area, Cherry Grove, was built sometime in the middle 1800's. Made of hewed logs, half of a log was cut out and the opening covered with greased paper. This let some light into the interior.

This primitive church served the community as both church and subscription school until the Antioch School was built in 1865. The Antioch School was then used for church services until the Antioch Church was built in 1883.

A few years later, some people decided to build a new Methodist church at Cherry Grove. During this church construction, an incident happened which has been told and retold down through the years.

Thomas Hartley, Jr. was known as an expert carpenter, so people expected he would get the contract to build the new Cherry Grove church. He apparently got paid in advance. The amount was four hundred dollars. Well, the way the story goes, he and his crew of workers were drinking as well as working. By the time quitting time came, they were feeling quite happy and looking for a joke to play. In the group there was a small man by the name of Ramsey. History doesn't say why he became their target but they decided to keep him from going home. They put him in a gunnysack (burlap bag) and hung the bag on a spike nail on the partially finished church wall. Then they all went home leaving him there. It was hours before someone passing on the road below heard his cries for help and rescued him.

This church was completed in 1894 and had a large congregation until one Sunday in May 1913 when a trash fire was built in the potbelly stove. Sparks from the chimney ignited the wood shingles and Cherry Grove burned to the ground and was never rebuilt.

At one time there had been a pretty Methodist Church on the left hand fork of Cow Run, near the head of the valley. The church, called Long Bottom, discontinued services in the 1930's and was torn down in the 1940's. In later years, there was another church on the left hand fork of Cow Run called Logger Head or by most people, the New Church. People came from miles around to attend meetings at this Church of God. Many did not come for religion, they came hoping to see a show, for this church's members were called Holy Rollers and they sometimes talked in unknown tongues and shouted and carried on.

Remember, church was a social thing as well as a religious thing; It was a chance to go somewhere, to get dressed up, to chat with neighbors and hear some news. People were just starved for entertainment.

Boys would walk for miles through fields; the roads were too muddy, to a church meeting that they thought a girl that they liked would be attending.

Boys filed into the church one after another and sat on the very back benches. Girls chose seats on the middle benches, occasionally stealing a glance back, making sure the boy they were interested in was there and hopefully would ask to walk her home.

The boys would sit for a while, then at an unseen signal, they would all rise and file outside. Occasionally you might catch a glimpse of a boy peering in a back window. After awhile, they would all come back in and sit down again. When the meeting was finally over, the girls hurriedly walked out the door to find a gauntlet of boys waiting. One boy after another sidled up to the girl he had been waiting all evening to ask that all-important question, "Kin I walk you home?" Sometimes the girl's home would be miles in the opposite direction from his home. So frequently it would be in the wee hours of the morning before the boy got home with only the memory of holding her hand as they walked.

Built in 1883, the Antioch United Brethren Church, like many others, was a simple rectangle with windows on each side, a door centered in front and a cupola on top. A raised platform ran across the end of the church with the pulpit in the center and a pump organ at one side. The seats were handmade poplar benches with angled comfortable backs. In early years, the church was lit with candles. In later years, an Aladdin lamp hung from the ceiling. There was some kind of apparatus by which it was lowered to be fueled and lit. A large potbelly stove with a coal pile just outside took care of heat.

This church was struck by lightening and burned in 1943. It was rebuilt in 1944.

Ice Cream Suppers

Sometime during the summer, must churches had an ice cream supper on the church grounds. The church building was not utilized in any way. The Antioch Church members would have thought that would have been sacrilege.

The event was always held on a Saturday evening in July or August. When the big day came, the entire community got busy. Worktables were borrowed from homes and some of the men built a temporary serving counter. Big blocks of ice had been ordered through a store in Cottageville and someone went after it, at the same time picking up two five gallon ice cram freezers that were always borrowed from either the Mason or Odd fellow lodge. Soft drinks always called "pop" were to be sold as well as candy bars and these were picked up too. The big blocks of ice were wrapped in burlap and pounded with hammers until the chunks were small enough to fit in the freezers.

Families brought milk, eggs, sugar and vanilla from home and mixed enough for the two five gallon freezers. Several families owned one-gallon freezers and they brought them with the ice cream already mixed, ready to be frozen. Different flavors were used such as chocolate, banana and strawberry.

A bag of coarse salt from the salt works at nearby Hartford, WV was used to alternate with ice layers in the freezers. The afternoon was spent taking turns cranking the ice cream freezers, occasionally adding more ice and salt as the mixture melted.

By the time five o'clock came, the ice cream was finished and covered well to keep it firm.

Of course, there was no electric but a church member, Hoyt Hartley, rigged an electric light bulb to run off a car battery. That, together with an Aladdin lamp, made plenty of light around the serving counter.

A nickel bought a generous dip of ice cream or an ice-cold bottle of pop kept in a large zinc washtub of ice and water. This was before plastic. The ice cream was served in paper dishes with tiny tin spoons.

There was light around the serving area but off to the side where we young folks were playing "Round" games, it was pretty dark but we didn't care because we seldom got together and we were having fun. "Chase the Buffalo" was one of the games. Some of the words to another game was "go in and out the window". We swung our partners as we sang the words and had a wonderful time. Sometimes there were so many of us we would have two games going.

Any kind of dancing was considered a deadly sin in the church community but thinking about it sixty years later it seems to me we were really dancing without the usual music. We just sang the music. I don't remember ever hearing any objections to the games but in discussing this recently with a childhood friend, I found out otherwise. She had participated in the games only once. Her parents found out and they both whipped her. I remember they were members of the "New Church" located on the left hand fork of Cow Run.

This once a year ice cream supper was the only fundraiser the church had.

Toward the end of the supper, donated cakes and pies were auctioned. Of course, some had been sold by the slice to people to eat with their ice cream.

I remember an incident that happened one time that had to do with the auction. Loraine Kerwood was a noted cook and baker and she always made a gorgeous layer cake with fluffy pink icing. Her cake always brought the highest price. It was an unspoken rule that her cake was not to be cut. It was always saved for the auction. Well, someone did cut a slice from it and when Loraine discovered it she threw a fit, in fact she raised such a commotion her husband, Raymond, had to come and settle her down. No one ever owned up to the terrible deed. Everybody was busy and no one had noticed.

Loraine has been gone for many years, I don't have her recipe for the gorgeous pink cake but I do have the recipe for her pecan pies, which are the best I've ever tried.

Loraine's Pecan Pie

2 unbaked 9-inch pie shells
1 cup sugar
1 tablespoon flour
5 eggs beaten
3 tablespoons melted butter
1 tablespoon vanilla
1 pint bottle clear Karo syrup
1 pinch salt
1 cup pecan pieces

Mix sugar and flour. Add to beaten eggs. Beat in all other ingredients except for pecans, which are stirred in last.

Pour into pie shells and bake in 375-degree oven, 40 to 50 minutes until filling is set. Cool. Cut each pie into 8 pieces and top each with a teaspoon of whipped cream.

Wash Day

In winter, a dreaded weekly job was Monday washday. The kettle stand stood outside the back yard gate. First you had to get a supply of wood and build a fire under it. Every family owned a brass or iron kettle which was placed on the stand and filled with water, a bucketful at a time, pumped from the well and carried across the yard and out the gate. We were lucky to have a copper wash boiler to heat the water in. When the water got hot, we dipped it out by the bucketful and carried it to the back porch and poured it into a Maytag gasoline powered wringer washer. A bar of P&G soap was shaved into pieces with a sharp knife and added to the washer with the white clothes. After the white things washed a while, they were run through the wringer into a galvanized washtub of warm rinse water. Then good colored clothes were put into the washer, then every day clothes and finally overalls, all using the same wash water. Sometimes, a second rinse water was used with bluing added. This made the white clothes whiter and every housewife wanted to get her clothes on the line first and wanted her white clothes to be the whitest.

Of course, just about everything but baby diapers had to be starched. Starch was made from a concoction of flour and water, cooked slightly, then when sufficiently thickened, it was diluted with water. Each piece of laundry was dipped in the starch and then put through the wringer, ready to be hung on the clothesline.

Making starch was somewhat easier if you could afford to buy the dark blue box of Argo starch, which most people had on their pantry shelf.

Sometimes it would be so cold; water splashed on the porch floor would freeze. Mom would heat the wooden clothespins in the oven so her hands wouldn't freeze to the clothes when she pinned them on the line. If it were very cold, the clothes would freeze instantly. A row of diapers would stand stiff in the wind like pennants on a ship. Diapers were used more than once. They were simply hung by the fire, dried and used again. Small infant's urine has no odor. There were no waterproof diaper covers so there was a lot of baby laundry. Boys wore dresses until they were toilet trained at about one year old. Babies that took much longer than that would have been considered "slow".

With all this Monday washing, the next day brought ironing. Everything was dampened down the night before. Items were spread out on a table. Dipping your hand into a bowl of warm water, you sprinkled each item, rolled it tightly and put it in a towel-lined basket. By morning, the clothes would be ready to iron. The ironing board was set up near the kitchen range and three insert irons were heated. Setting an iron holder down on the iron insert, you pushed a lever, which held the iron in place. You ironed with this one until it began to cool. Then you set the iron back on the stove, pushed a lever to release it and picked up a hot iron and repeated this until the ironing was finished. This usually made a hard days work.

The copper wash boiler did double duty. In the summer, it was used for canning called "cold packing". Daddy had made a wooden rack to fit in the bottom of the boiler. This prevented the glass canning jars from touching the bottom where they would have broken. The quart canning jars fit neatly in the wash boiler. Water was carried to cover the jars completely and a fire built. When the water boiled, you could start timing. Green beans took three hours. Meat took four hours. The water had to be boiling constantly so that required frequent attention to keep the fire "just so".

Children's Day

Back then in the 30's, Father's Day was unheard of but mothers were honored on the second Sunday in May by everyone wearing either a red or white flower to church. The color worn depended on whether the mother was living or not.

Children's Day was the second Sunday in June. Now that was a big event. Every church had a program with each and every child having a part. Some of the women would meet with the children at the church for several afternoons to practice, practice, practice. We practiced poems, little plays and best of all, drills, lots of intricate, precision, marching drills. We were so proud when we mastered the steps in unison.

When I was about eight or nine, our mothers made each of us a different colored crepe paper dress, complete with a ruffled neckline to wear in our drill.

The raised platform across the end of the church became a stage complete with curtains. Sheets were hung by large safety pins, which slid easily on a wire strung across the front of the "stage". The church would be decorated with armloads of wild pink roses and lots of greenery.

Visitors, coming to see the program, filled the church. I remember one Children's Day when the lamps were extinguished and the curtains were opened to reveal some of the older girls dressed in white robes forming a motionless tableau with flash powder burning. That was the wonderful final act and the surprised audience burst into wild applause.

Molasses Time

The days were getting shorter. Fall, with all its work preparing for the coming winter, was just around the corner. One job in particular I think folks actually looked forward to doing was the every fall ritual of making sorghum molasses. It was a lot of work but it was fun.

When the ground had warmed in the spring, the cane seed had been planted, carefully, three or four inches apart. The cane stalk needed this much room to grow fat and juicy. When the bushy seed heads of cane turned brown in early fall, it indicated the cane was ripe and ready for molasses making.

The cane seed heads would be topped and the blades stripped from the stalk as it was cut with a machete or possibly a corn cutter. It was stacked by the cane mill and was fed into the mill by the armload. The old horse just plodded around and around turning the mill and forcing the juice from the grinding cane stalks. The rich juice poured into a barrel. Then it was strained through cheesecloth and poured into the first section of the big molasses pan, which had just had water run through it. They did this water ritual every day to start the molasses making. The big molasses pan had sections with gates between them. It all started with the green juice fresh from the cane mill. It was cooked as it slowly moved from one section to another until it finally got to the last section where the finished product was strained and poured into jars.

The different sections were stirred with handmade wooden paddles and each section of cooking molasses had to have the foam skimmed from it, time after time. From the green molasses of the first section, which had just started to cook, to the last gated section, which would soon be ready to jar, there was much foam that needed to be skimmed. They always had a skimming hole. This hole was about thirty-six inches or more wide and quite deep. It was dug beside the furnace in easy flipping distance of the person in charge of skimming.

As you skimmed each section with a wooden skimmer, with a twist of your wrist you deposited the skimmings in the hole. If you made a large amount of molasses, the hole would eventually fill up and you would have to dip out the contents. This was not an envied job!

Hazel Hughes Sayre, whose father, "Bige", always made molasses, told me that her father once hurriedly tossed a bucket of green skimmings into a nearby fishpond. She laughed as she told me, "Every fish died!"

Hazel is noted for her expertise in making molasses. Her father taught her well. She has made molasses all her life. She says it was hard work but she loved every minute of it. At the moment, she is a young 95 years old.

The fire in the furnace had to be tended carefully. Furnace is what they called the brick fire chamber they had made. That was an art in itself, constructing the furnace so it would draw right. The molasses pan, with its different sections of bubbling molasses, sat snugly on top of the brick "furnace".

When word got around by the Citizen Telephone party line that a neighbor was going to make molasses, we children clambered to go watch. We loved it, we ran around playing, laughing, hollering and probably getting in the way. One thing, the grownups were always hollering at any molasses making was, "Watch out, don't fall in the skimming hole!" I never actually knew of anyone falling in, although they were always joking about it and threatening someone with that very messy fate. I asked Hazel if anyone ever fell in the skimming hole and she said "Oh land, yes and what a mess!"

Neighbors were always dropping by, meeting other neighbors and joking, always joking; perhaps about the consistency of the finished product, perhaps about the skimming hole. They were always joking about that skimming hole.

So many people came to watch the molasses making that some makers kept a guest book for visitors to sign. We children liked to get a short length of cane stalk and dip it in the bubbling molasses and then we licked it off.

Sometimes unexpected problems arose. One former molasses maker, Naomi Knopp, told me she had had to put up a tent to protect herself from a swarm of hungry yellow jackets that insisted on helping her jar molasses!

We frequently ate sorghum molasses for breakfast. We poured two or three spoonfuls on our plate, in a puddle and added a little chunk of butter. We stirred the resulting mixture until it was mixed well, then we spread that mixture on mom's hot soda biscuits. That was so good!

The other way I liked molasses was in:

Molasses Cookies

1/2 cup shortening
1 cup sugar

2 eggs
1/2 cup milk
1/2 cup molasses

3 cups flour
3 teaspoons baking
powder
1 teaspoon cinnamon
1 teaspoon cloves
3/4 cup raisins

Beat the shortening and sugar to a cream; add the well-beaten eggs, then the milk, molasses and raisins, and lastly the dry ingredients well sifted together. Drop by spoonfuls on greased pans some distance apart. Bake about ten minutes in a moderate oven.

Dark Gingerbread

1/2 cup shortening
1 cup molasses
1 egg
2 tablespoons milk
2 teaspoons baking powder

2 cups flour
1/2 teaspoon salt
2 teaspoons ginger

Heat the shortening till hissing; pour it into a bowl in which the molasses has already been measured. Add the egg and milk and mix lightly. Sift together the flour, salt, ginger and baking powder, and stir into the liquid ingredients, beating and stirring only enough to blend. Pour in two shallow well-greased pans and bake twenty minutes in a moderately hot oven.

These molasses recipes are from a 1908 cookbook I grew up using. Keep in mind, there were no electric mixers and no heat gauges on ovens then.

The Silvertone Radio

We came home from school one day to find Daddy unpacking a beautiful cathedral style Silvertone radio that our mailman and his horse had delivered. We were so excited; we thought we would be listening to *Jack Armstrong* and *Little Orphan Annie* that very evening. But such was not to be. Sears and Roebuck had made a mistake. They had sent a 110 volt radio instead of a 32 volt that daddy had ordered. Of course it wouldn't work so it was repacked and given to our poor mailman to return. Four days later he brought the 32-volt radio and we enjoyed many hours of good listening.

My father was not a sports fan but neighbors on up the valley were. I doubt Daddy even knew about the big heavyweight world championship fight between Joe Louis and Max Schneling until Tom Sayre and his three sons, Quentin, Ralph, and Don came to our house one evening wanting to listen to the big fight, their radio wasn't working. Of course, we all listened to the fight even if we didn't know what the sports announcers were talking about!

Rural mail carriers were overworked and under appreciated. Our mailman from the time I could remember was Tuncil Wright. He traversed the entire Cow Run valley. He kept an extra horse at Wedges on Route 87 so he could change horses when his load was excessive. He sometimes drove a huge wheel one-horse cart when he had even more packages. There was a weight limit of seventy pounds on each package. In addition to regular mail, there might be a case of thirty dozen eggs and possibly a cream can or two.

Winter was bad with the fetlock deep red clay mud making a sucking sound at each step of the horse. At times, the horse was so overloaded the mailman walked instead of riding until he delivered enough of the load and made room to climb into thc saddle and ride.

Catalogs were dreaded by mail carriers and eagerly anticipated by his customers. We spent many evenings turning pages in the wish books. Whether it was Sears Roebuck, Montgomery Ward or Alden's, it had better be delivered the same day as your neighbors. If you got a catalog one day and mine didn't come until a day or two later, a complaint might be filed with the post office. An earlier mailman was said to have been fired when it became known he had dumped a load of catalogs off the iron bridge into Cow Run.

Looking back it seems amazing how wonderful the mail service was. For instance, if you put an order to Sears and Roebuck in your mailbox on Monday, you could expect your order on Thursday. Montgomery Ward was even quicker. An order placed on Monday would be received on Wednesday. Philadelphia was Sears and Roebuck's head quarters, Baltimore was Montgomery Wards.

The railroads were responsible for this quick service. The Ohio River Railroad had been built in 1885 and 1886. It connected Parkersburg and Huntington. This was soon followed by a branch-line connecting Millwood, Cottageville, Angerona, Evans and Ripley. You could board a train at Ripley in early morning and be in Parkersburg by 9:00 a.m.

There was a mail car on every train with clerks busily sorting the mail.

The Jackson County Fair

The Jackson County Fair was the big event of the year. Started in 1877 in Ripley, the fair grew over the years and became the best county fair in the state. Situated in an oak grove on Cunningham land, near Evans, the fairground was a wonderland for children. We were just turned loose. There was no thought of danger. We walked from one end of the fairground to the other a dozen times a day. We walked through the cattle barn; we walked through the horse barn, through the sheep barn, through the hog barn etc. We would check out the blue ribbon winners and see if we agreed with the judges' choices. In the middle of the fairground set the exhibit hall. All kinds of fresh fruits and vegetables were here. There were rows of canned items and displays of sewing, quilting, knitting, etc. There was much competition in getting award-winning ribbons and if you got a blue ribbon you were very proud!

Mom entered an infant's long christening gown. It had exquisite embroidered work. She was noted as a top seamstress so when she just got second place she was disappointed. After looking at the blue ribbon first place award and seeing it was poorly made, she never entered anything in the fair again.

This was probably the year the story went around about a jar of canned chicken. It seems this jar of chicken got a first place award and the recipient was so pleased she presented the jar of chicken to the judge. The trouble was, when the jar was opened they had to bury the chicken and the jar!

At the fair, farmers could enter a basket or box of things grown on their farm, the more things the better. I remember the Ray Hartley family winning first place. I can't remember any of the many things they displayed except for one. Some branches of honey locust showing their long three and four inch shiny thorns were used.

There were horse races every day together with sulky races. The racehorse stables were way back in the field on the right side of the fairgrounds. Sometimes we walked way back there. All the horses had their heads out over their half doors just waiting until it was time for their next race.

We kids watched the races but what we really liked were the stage shows in the center of the racetrack. The entertainment I liked best was an acrobatic show featuring two little girls, my age, dressed in red spangled leotards, performing on a trapeze bar. Oh, how I envied them. I wanted to do that!

One night of the fair they would set off fireworks in the center of the racetrack. The bleachers would be full of people oohing and aahing as they watched the display. I remember they finished with a huge firework American Flag.

There were always gypsies at the fair with their colorful clothes and covered wagons. We were fascinated and half-afraid of them as we watched, from a distance, the gypsy fortune-teller try to entice someone to enter her tent.

At the far end of the fair grounds, the Cunninghams had an open-air beer garden complete with a nickelodeon, which played the Beer Barrel Polka almost continuously.

At the other end of the fair grounds were the Hootsie Cootsie dancing girls. There, three fading beauties with their gauzy rhinestone studded, low-cut costumes, which were a little, bedraggled and dusty would come out of their tent. When a crowd gathered one of the girls would do a tantalizing bit of a belly dance. Then the three girls would retreat to their tent and the barker would take over and loudly exhort the men to spend a quarter to go in and see the wonders of the universe! The men looked sheepish when they went in and even more so when they came out.

At the left end of the fairgrounds was a long low building with a sawdust floor sheltering a row of pit toilets; these were the women's rest rooms. Our mothers' were always warning, "don't sit down on the seat, don't touch anything…you'll get the "Bad Disease."" Of course there was no place to wash your hands although there was a drilled well with a pump on the fairgrounds.

A mentally challenged woman worked cleaning. Looking back I think she was hoping for tips but sadly I never saw anyone tip her.

All carnival rides were a dime except for the Merry Go Round, which was a nickel. We children loved to watch the rides even though we didn't have money to ride ourselves. This was during the 30's and the Great Depression stalked the land. We were lucky our parents could rake up the change to pay our way into the fair and we had a wonderful time enjoying all the different sights and sounds. My granddad, G.W. Sayre, "Pap George" was in his eighties and I was seven or eight when he came to the fair. I was thrilled when he bought two tickets to take me on the Merry Go Round. Granddad with the aid of his two canes climbed aboard, and then we walked to the nearest fancy bench and sat down. I was disappointed that we were not going to ride the beautiful carousel horses. I was much too shy to say anything but perhaps he saw my face. Anyway he got up and we climbed on two horses and around and around we went up and down side by side on the Merry Go Round I will never forget how happy I was. Some onlookers gathered, pointing to the elderly man with a long white beard and two canes riding a carousel horse on the merry-go-round.

Big old oak trees sheltered the fairgrounds. An ice cream sandwich vendor who was obviously bored kept looking up through the tree branches and saying things like "There it is"! He soon had a crowd looking up in the oak trees, looking for they didn't know what. Daddy caught on right away and helped him, pointing as if he saw something. The crowd grew larger with everybody craning their necks. It was funny!

We were going to ride the Ferris wheel! My cousin Ocie Marx and her son Douglas, who was exactly my age, were visiting us for the summer and we had come to the fair together. They had bought our Ferris wheel tickets and we had felt so grown up giving them to the ticket taker and climbing into the swinging seat without a grownup going with us. Then we were off! The seat was moving higher and higher. We could see the tops of the tents on the midway and hear the chants of the barkers as their voices floated upward. We've stopped! The seat we're in hangs motionless as do all the other seats. We are stuck about half way to the top. I'm enjoying this. Everybody is looking at the Ferris wheel and its captives. As we sit there just hanging in the air, I'm thinking what a story I'll have to tell the other kids, "How I got stuck on the Ferris wheel". Our parents are down below wearing worried looks. Now it's started, once again we are moving and I'm wishing we had been stuck longer. Up, up we go until we're on the very top. Then we stop again! This time several minutes tick by before the big Ferris wheel engine coughs and springs to life. Down, down we come until we're on the ground again.

Most country people took a picnic lunch when they went to the fair. Then the family met at their vehicle, car or wagon, at noon and ate together. Usually country ham, fried chicken, homemade bread with real cow butter, blackberry jelly, chocolate cake and apple pie .I was tired of this kind of food and would have preferred the hot dogs and hamburgers sold on the fairgrounds. Looking back I'm sure the fair people would have preferred ours.

This chocolate cake was the one we would have had in our picnic lunch at the fair. It always was our favorite. The recipe was featured in a farm magazine in the 1930's.

Best Chocolate Cake
1/2 cup plus 1 tablespoon shortening
1 1/2 cups sugar
2 eggs
2 cups sifted cake flour
4 tablespoons cocoa
2 tablespoons hot water
1 1/8 teaspoon baking soda
1 cup buttermilk

1 teaspoon salt

1 tablespoon vanilla

Cream sugar, shortening, salt and vanilla for 3 minutes. Add hot water, beat one minute. Add eggs, one at a time, beating well after each. Sift flour, cocoa and soda. Add, alternately with buttermilk, beating well.

Pour batter into two 8 or 9 inch cake pans lined with greased wax paper. Bake at 350 degrees for 30 minutes or until cake tests done.

Mocha Frosting

2 cups confectioners' sugar

3 tablespoons cocoa

1/8 teaspoons salt

3 tablespoons butter

1 teaspoon vanilla

3 tablespoons cold strong coffee

Sift confectioner's sugar, cocoa, and salt. Cream butter in a two-quart bowl. Add 4 tablespoons of sifted mixture to butter. Beat well. Add vanilla and beat. Add rest of dry mixture alternately with cold coffee. Beat for several minutes to incorporate air into frosting. Fill and frost cake.

Note: If using regular flour instead of cake flour, deduct 2 tablespoons from each cup.

Free Delivery

There was one wonderful convenience we country residents had and I'm sure other communities shared in this. I'm talking about free delivery of everything from a sack of chicken feed to 3 cents worth of yeast, which, believe it or not, I've ordered many a time. Anyway, there were three grocery general stores in Cottageville and each store "run a route" out Cow Run once a week. Dan

McDermott, L.O. Hunt, and John Kerwood were the owners of the three stores. Each store route was on a different day. You made a list of your wants on the back of a penny postcard and mailed it to the store. They would bring the things you ordered and pick up your eggs and perhaps a can of cream. You could order anything the stores carried. Once we ordered a twenty-five pound block of ice to make a freezer of ice cream. Now the grocer would have had to order the ice from an ice company.

In addition to these country routes, John Kerwood drove many miles above Charleston to the coal mining region to deliver eggs to them. John Kerwood was not a large man but he would hoist a hundred pound bag of laying mash on his shoulder and walk to the big chicken house Daddy had had built several years before his death. John would put the sack of mash in the feed room and leave it up to us to get it open. Now that was a job itself. The brightly colored printed bags were simply rectangles sewn together with string. You worked on the top seam until you got a string end, then you pulled. Now if you got the right one, the seam came undone like magic. Usually it wasn't that easy and you would have to try again.

Maggy Kerwood was John's mother and she frequently went on the route with him. I'm sure she was a big help with the paperwork, checking off groceries as they delivered them. On, John's route was an eccentric man by the name of Anderson who lived in the head of a holler on the left hand fork of Cow Run. He had the reputation of going without clothes and sure enough there he was, naked except for a piece of a burlap bag, which he was wearing like an apron! Maggy just laughed about it. It didn't bother her.

Blackberry Pickin'

Blackberries were an essential part of the winter's food supply. When the berries ripened, everyone who was able headed for the blackberry patch. Even small children picked. A neighbor told her brood that the sweat bees were biting because they weren't picking fast enough! Another neighbor who kept a hired hand paid him to join them in the berry patch. A large family with several pickers might take a washtub to the berry patch. As each person filled his bucket, he emptied it into the tub and started picking again. Often the mother stayed home to can berries on a coal and wood range, which heated her kitchen to well over a hundred degrees. Families bragged about how many quarts they had canned.

Most farms had some wasteland that sheltered wild blackberries. If they did not, they tried to find someone who wasn't using all theirs and asked to pick. We did not have a single berry brier on our farm because every so often daddy would walk the fields with a grubbing hoe and get rid of any briers, thistles and sprouts that dared showed themselves. So our berries were picked on one of my grandfather's farms. Each day daddy would take two ten-quart *Wearever* kettles (I still have one) and drive our Model T Ford a mile to Sayre Hollow. Mom would stay home and can the previous day's yields. Daddy had short, stubby fingers and even though he never ate a berry, Mom, with her small nimble fingers could out pick him and still eat all she wanted. She actually liked picking berries. I was little, about five or six, and didn't have to go but each morning, forgetting how miserable I had been the day before, I begged to go again. If I went I had to take a pint-measuring cup and pick it full of berries before I could quit and play. I thought I would never get that cup full. The sweat bees would get after me. The tall grass made me itch. I would get thirsty and it would be a long way to the Model

T car and the drinking water. Then I would spill my berries and have to pick them up and pick some more until I got that cup full again. Then I would have to wait and wait until daddy picked both his big kettles full.

Then we went home to a fresh from the garden dinner, green beans cooked with pork side meat, creamed new potatoes, wilted lettuce, sliced tomatoes and best of all, Blackberry Cobbler. First before we ate we had to discard our berry picking clothes and take sponge baths to get rid of the awful chiggers. Some always survived and made life miserable, as we scratched chigger bites day and night.

Blackberry Cobbler meant different things to different people. In our neighborhood it meant a quick cobbled together recipe of berries, sugar and dough. A busy housewife canning berries, tending her garden and cooking for a family did not have time to fool with pies. She simply took a large bread pan, lined it with pie dough, poured some berries in, put some sugar on top and added a top crust. Nothing was measured. It was baked in a hot oven until the crust was golden and berry juice was bubbling out. The cobbler was dipped out with a large spoon into cereal bowls. Some people put cream on top but most ate the delicious juicy cobbler plain.

Cobbler Recipes

Blackberry Cobbler
8 cups blackberries
2 ½ cups sugar

Rhubarb Cobbler
8 cups Rhubarb
4 cups sugar

Gooseberry Cobbler
8 cups gooseberries
3 ½ cups sugar

For each 9 by 13 baking dish use any pastry recipe making the amount you would need for three 9-inch single piecrusts. After you mix dough divide in half and roll out for the top and bottom cobbler crust.

Blackberry Cake

I was twelve and looking for something to read at my Uncle Harve and Aunt Arkie's house. I was standing on a press back kitchen chair rummaging through some old books on the top shelve of a closet. Reading material was scarce, there was no county library and I had read the few books we had at our one room school again and again. I was always looking for something to read and something different to bake so I was delighted when by standing on tiptoe I could reach the farthest corner where there was an old tattered cookbook. In it I found a recipe for blackberry cake. We always had canned berries in the cellar so I tried the cake and it became a family favorite. Here is the recipe. Read it carefully!

Blackberry Cake
1 cup butter
2 cups sugar
5 eggs
8 tablespoons sour milk
1 teaspoon soda
2 teaspoons baking powder
1 teaspoon vanilla
1 teaspoon cinnamon
1 teaspoon nutmeg
1 teaspoon cloves
1½ cups drained blackberries
Flour to make a batter
Combine butter and sugar thoroughly. Add beaten eggs. Dissolve soda in sour milk and add alternately with dry ingredients, which have been sifted together. Add vanilla

and blackberries. Stir, and if necessary add a little more flour.

Bake in layers and put together with frosting.

This frosting recipe was in a Rumford Baking Powder cookbook published in the 1930's. I usually used it for this cake.

Caramel Frosting
1 ½ cups brown sugar
¾ cup cream or milk
1 tablespoon butter
1 teaspoon vanilla

Put the sugar, cream (or milk) and butter into a saucepan and cook gently till a little dropped in coldwater forms a soft ball. Remove from the fire, cool, add the flavoring, and beat until think enough to spread.

Summer Time

Summer time was barefoot time. We kids looked forward to what we called "pullin off barefoot". We all wanted to be the first and started begging our parents for permission as soon as the middle of April arrived. The Hartley twins, Alice and Anna, always had to wait until May regardless of the weather.

We never wore shoes in summer except to church or to town.

From the dew heavy grass of morning to the velvety road dust, it all felt delightful to feet newly released from the confines of heavy shoes.

The soles of our feet got tough. Sometimes I got a stubbed toe and sometimes asked for help to pick out a stubborn thorn or sand brier with a sewing needle.

I always had to go around the church hill, find the cows and drive them to the barn for milking. As long as I stayed on the cow path, I was all right my feet were fine, but if I had to get a switch and go after a reluctant cow, I had to get off the path and deal with sand briers. I learned that if I ran fast through them I was less likely to get some in my feet. The last thing before bedtime, I had to get a wash pan of water and sitting on the back steps, I washed my feet.

I always enjoyed that walk around the hill. As I returned with the cows in the evening a spectacular sunset framed a lone house on the crest of a high ridge in the distance. I always wanted to go there, to that big house and look down the valley to see how our home looked from there.

Many years later I was with a couple and we were driving around the county stopping at homes and asking for donations to rebuild the Antioch Church which had been struck by lightening and burned. I kept a careful list of the donations. I remember one woman living in a shack gave us five cents. I hope it wasn't her last nickel but I'm afraid it was.

We were on unfamiliar roads to me. We drove out a long ridge and stopped at a big house. I got out of the vehicle and turned around. There it was, the long sweeping valley at my feet! I was at the big house I had dreamed of visiting when I was a little girl driving the cows to the barn for milking.

There in the distance, looking like a child's toy was the Antioch Church. I could see my home, the big white house and the red barn. There was the road curling down the hill past the neighbors. There was Ray Hartley's and Ether Hunts' and the yellow tile blockhouse John Hartley had built to replace the historic old home his grandfather had built when he came to this valley about 1850. That wonderful old home had been struck by lightening and burned when I was twelve years old. I still remember its high fireplace you could stand up in. Then there was Tom and Florence Sayre's neat white house and nestled, at the very foot of the ridge, the log cabin where Tom's parents Abijah and Ellen Hartley Sayre had lived and raised their family, never dreaming that some day their log home would be moved to become the focal point of Ravenswood Riverfront Park. I'll always remember that day and the view that I finally got to see.

Across the big bottom cornfield lie Cow Run and there was a large enough hole of water that we called it the deep hole. At one place where the roots of a big sycamore extended out over the water it was actually over our heads. The hole of water wasn't very wide but it felt wonderful to get on some old clothes and jump into that cool water, especially if you had spent the day hoeing corn for the big wage of 10 cents a day.

I could neither swim nor float but it was fun to dog paddle and splash around. Only once do I remember my dad joining me, he had on bib overalls and floated effortlessly in the center of the swimming hole.

Summer time meant mulberry time. Mulberries ripened from a pale green to a light red, then a red and finally a luscious purple. We children had a feast. Every evening after work found us climbing around the small trees that grew against the bank directly across the road from our house. I was alone climbing, directly above a barbed wire fence when I slipped and fell. Of course, I landed on the fence. I ran to the house, bleeding and crying. I do not remember how mom doctored me. She always kept a supply of "finger stalls" she had made to take care of cut and burned fingers, both very common on a farm. The fingerstalls were sewn to look like miniature pillowcases with a narrow strip of cloth, attached to tie the contraption over a bandaged finger. With her supply of fingerstalls, mom kept soft worn out strips of muslin sheets for bandages. I do know I had scars from the barbed wire encounter for years, until they became lost in my many stretch mark scars.

I remember neighbors spreading an old white sheet under a mulberry tree and then shaking the tree to get mulberries to can since, for some reason, there were few blackberries that year.

Another treat we children liked in the summer was little green apples. Up the road past our house was a common apple tree. It was growing right beside the road and year after year it produced lots of little green apples, which we ate with coarse salt. They were only about an inch and a half across when we began eating them. We threw sticks and rocks into the tree to bring them down. In spite of their reputation, I never heard of anyone becoming ill from eating them. Perhaps it was the salt we always ate with them or perhaps we had "cast iron stomachs".

The apple tree was right beside the road and we were there a lot. If we heard a car coming, we ran and hid in the brush. This was at the time of the Lindbergh baby kidnapping and we were scared of being kidnapped!

There were so few cars that we knew the sound of some. A child would holler, "here comes John Kerwood", and we would scramble for the brush. John would go flying by, not knowing all the eyes that were watching him!

In late September there was another delicious treat waiting for us. In some states they are called custard apples. Here we just called them Paw Paws. The tasty yellow flesh looks like, feels like and tastes like custard. They have large shiny black, flat seeds, which can be used in crafts. Most people just eat them as is, but I have found they enhance many recipes. Yeast breads, breakfast muffins, desserts, cookies, or cakes, Paw Paws blend with them all.

In late October, depending on whether there had been a hard frost came our last treat of the year, persimmons. Some trees bear better tasting fruit than others so you need to find one that is really good and visit that tree every year. Persimmons aren't good until after a hard frost so wait until then before you start looking and tasting.

Chamber Pot Beans

Okey, "Oke", and Diana "Annie" Crum had a nice farm with a big two story white house, which they filled with fourteen children, thirteen boys and one girl!

Cash money was short and Dr. Harrison charged $5.00 to come from Cottageville, usually in the middle of the night to deliver a baby. Annie was my father's sister so they would come to him to borrow the money to pay the doctor. Sometimes they would just get him paid back, a little at a time, and here would come another baby and another $5.00 loan!

Some of the boys left home and became teachers. The girl, Clara, became a teacher in the Roanoke, Virginia School system.

After Oak and Annie were gone, some of the boys continued to work the farm. They would put a pot of beans on the stove to simmer so they would be done when they came in tired and hungry. This is how it was said they cooked the beans:

Take one brand new enamelware chamber pot and add a pound of dry beans, any kind, which have been rinsed and soaked overnight in water to cover and then drained.

Add a ¼ lb. of side meat or ham, cut into one to two inch cubes, and a little salt and pepper to taste. Cover with lots of water and place on middle of range and let them simmer all day. Cooked in a chamber pot, the beans would not boil over as would probably have happened with a conventional pan.

The Floods

The backwater was coming, backwater from the Ohio River. The date was March 1936. They said we were going to have a flood. Each day, the water crept higher and higher. A stick placed at the water's edge each night would be some feet out in the water when morning came. Cow Run's lower bottoms were soon covered and the roads cut off. We kids enjoyed the excitement. There was no danger of any of the homes on Cow Run having water damage. They were all built on higher ground.

Edward Hartley and Roy Shinn each built a john boat and fashioned some oars. Using a boat, the Hartley's could reach their upper farm, two miles on up the valley.

One Sunday afternoon, we young people all got together; we were going to go see the high water. We told our parents and surprisingly, no one stopped us. We met at the lower end of our orchard, at the big oak tree. That's where the water had stopped. The two boys with their homemade johnboats ferried us across our big low bottom of floodwater. None of us had ever been in any kind of boat before and we sat very still out in the middle of all that water. There wasn't a ripple. Just perfectly flat and motionless muddy water. Cow Run itself was under there somewhere. Then I realized you could tell where by the rows of treetops sticking out of the water on each side of the creek, marking its location. The boys had to navigate carefully through these tree branches. When we got to the far side, they tied up the boats and we started walking, heading for the top of Angerona Hill, the highest land around; and there it was, the scene we had walked so far to see. We stared in awe at the water. Water everywhere. There were flooded valleys in all directions, as far as the eye could see. We could see an occasional stove pipe sticking up out of the water and realized there was a house submerged under each one. It was unbelievable. We walked somberly back down the long path. For the first time, I felt afraid. We loaded up the boats and went back across to dry land. It took more than one trip to get us all back. We were thrilled, we had got to see the high water, and we talked about it to anyone who would listen. After all these years, I still remember what I wore on that rowboat trip. I had saved thirty-three cents and I ordered a jacket from the catalog, Alden's, I think. I was so proud of my new jacket; it was royal blue and looked like suede but wore like paper! It soon tore up. Even with everything so cheap during the depression, thirty-three cents didn't buy a very durable jacket!

The 1936 flood was not nearly as high as the 1913 flood. That's what old timers told us as they pointed out a little block of wood high in a tree. It seems Henry Hartley had rowed a boat around during the height of the 1913 flood, and nailed little blocks of wood on trees showing where the floodwaters reached. I can remember one high on a tree at the iron bridge and one on a tree on a wooded road bank between our house and Ether Hunts home. There were others. We found it hard to believe that the 1913 flood was so much higher than the 1936 flood we had just endured. As flood talk gradually died away as the main topic of conversation, we never dreamed that in less than a year we would be facing a huge flood rivaling that of 1913. The 1936 flood had covered bottoms and valleys. The January 1937 flood seemed to cover everything as the water snaked up every little hollow. Still no homes on Cow Run were endangered. Much later we found out that in some localities the 1937 flood had tied the 1913 flood and in some places, it had exceeded it.

During the 1937 flood, I was outside in our yard when I heard a boat coming up the valley through our bottoms. I watched as a large Coast Guard cabin cruiser went by, on its way up the valley, speeding over cornfields now covered with several feet of floodwater. They soon realized their mistake. They made a sweeping turn throwing up a spray of water and back down the valley they came. I watched as they sped over our fields until they disappeared from my sight where the valley curved. We heard later the Coast Guard boat was taking mail to Evans and became lost. The flooded Mill Creek Valley would have taken them to Evans. At some place, they had turned right and followed Cow Run valley.

My cousin, Dorothy Baker Hamilton, who as a young girl lived between Cottageville and Evans, says that during the 1937 flood, a man named Hans Morgan delivered Storks bread by boat to families held prisoner by the flood. This was a godsend for many.

Many years before, during the 1913 flood, a tragedy happened in the village of Angerona as an indirect result of the flood. The Ong family, who had founded the town, knew the rising waters would soon come to their house so they were in the process of moving the furniture from the first to the second floor of the big home when a piano fell on one of the Ong men, killing him. Also during the 1913 flood, there is a true tale with a happier ending. Clara Capehart, a ninety two year old resident of Letart, told me the story that her father, William Rollins had told her. Letart was an Ohio River town and during the 1913 flood with the Ohio so high and wild, almost anything could be seen floating by. A church from Millwood with a rooster perched on the cupola went by but when William saw the house floating toward him he enlisted the help of his brother, Joe Rollins to try and capture it and capture it they did. William Rollins raised his growing family there. He had two children when he got the flood house and three more, including Clara, were born in the house! The flood house is still standing in Letart after nearly a hundred years. Drop by Clara's sometime and she will point it out to you.

Clara told me this story about how she attended high school. During the 1930's there was a ferryboat running between Letart and Letart Falls directly across the Ohio River. So Clara rode the ferry morning and evening in order to go to high school in Letart Falls. She was frequently the only passenger. If it was very, very cold and there were chunks of ice floating in the river, the ferryman would station her at the rail in the front of the boat and give her a long pole to push the ice chunks away! Now that was a different kind of transportation for a student!

The Gigantic Boat in the Cornfield

It was March 1910. There she was, 235 feet long with a 190-foot luxury cabin containing fifty staterooms. Paneled walls in exotic woods, beveled mirrors, and a floor covered with a midnight blue embroidered velvet carpet, all spelled money. At a time when towns didn't even have electric lights, this palace steamer had a large electric plant and was lit up with lots of lights from top to bottom. People were so enthused about the electric lights that they would build bonfires by the river and sit and watch for the huge boat to pass, if they heard it was in the area. She made an impressive display, especially to people who had never seen an electric light.

This steamer, the *Virginia*, was a floating palace. Only she wasn't floating. That was the trouble. She was stuck fast on an Indian mound, 600 feet from the Ohio River in the middle of Jim Williamson's very muddy cornfield.

The *Virginia* became an instant tourist attraction. A surrey with a fringe on top brought loads of sightseers from Ravenswood, only seven miles away, to view the stranded steamboat. The railroads ran special excursion trains to the site and much smaller steamers brought people from Gallipolis and Parkersburg. Everyone wanted to see for themselves. They thought it better than a showboat or a circus. This was different. It was a sight you'd never see again.

The *Virginia* belonged to a large steamship company in Pittsburgh that was in deep financial trouble. At this time there were no locks and dams on the Ohio River and it had been a dry year. The river had not had enough water in places to float the huge boat. Finally, the spring rains came and they decided to send her down the river. So with a load of 600 tons of cargo, fifty-four passengers and a crew of thirty, she headed for New Orleans.

Heavy rains brought the Ohio River to flood stage. Lights along the shore to help pilots stay in the channel were all under water and the boat crew was on their own. They landed freight at Ravenswood and found a passenger who wanted to buy a ticket to Willow Grove, just seven miles down the river, where the aluminum plant is now.

The pilot of the boat said it was too dangerous to try to stop at Willow Grove. The boat captain overruled him. When they stopped, the current was so swift it caught the steamer and swept it into the cornfield. All attempts to free it failed and there it stayed until June when the rains came again and finally the *Virginia* was free.

Williamson couldn't plant corn so he attempted to collect rent for the *Virginia* occupying his farmland!

Cow Run's Silver Dream

My little legs were tired and so were other students. It was my first year of school and on this pretty fall day, classes had been dismissed for the afternoon and we were going on a hike to the old silver mine. We were all delighted; a hike was a rare treat. Our one room school was called Silver Valley and my daddy, John J. Sayre, was the teacher. I was disappointed when we finally got to the mine's old location. It had been over 50 years since the shaft had been sunk and there wasn't much to see, just a big hole or depression in the ground about the size of a small house with brush growing thickly all over it.

A silver mine on Cow Run, unbelievable! Well believe it. It actually happened. In the years after the Civil War, men were dreaming big dreams and big schemes. Men not only believed that veins of silver ore were hiding under the red clay of Jackson County hills; they spent thousands of dollars in sinking shafts, hundreds of feet deep in search of the precious metal. The search for silver in this area was not made by simple uneducated folk, but by hardheaded businessmen who apparently believed in the knowledgeable geologists and chemists they had hired. No less than three separate mining companies were formed for the purpose of leasing land for silver exploration. They were the Pittsburgh Exploring, Developing and Mining Company; The Pomeroy Silver Mining Company; and the Point Pleasant Silver Mining and Exploring Company.

Some prominent people whose lands were leased were David Woodruff and wife, Elijah Staats and wife, Benjamin Flowers and wife, Abijah Hunt and wife, and Thomas Hartley. These leases may be seen in the Jackson County Courthouse at Ripley.

Great excitement was created by the report that silver had been found on Big Mill Creek about a mile from the village of Angerona. A company of Pittsburgh capitalists hurriedly organized to develop this Eldorado. After a shaft had been sunk to 400 feet and several entries driven, the silver dream evaporated, for they found nothing. This operation was called the Woodruff shaft since the Woodruff family owned the property.

About this time, another shaft was put down on a farm owned by Albert Shinn on Cow Run, Union District, Jackson County, one mile and half from Angerona but in the opposite direction from the Woodruff shaft. No silver was found and this shaft too was abandoned. The area around the old Shinn shaft located on the left hand fork of Cow Run is still called Silver Valley, although only the old timers know why.

Before all these happenings, records show a well was driven on the Woodruff property to a depth of 400 feet to check for salt water. Supposedly some silver ore had been found, which was sent away to be tested. It was found to be rich in silver.

Later rumors circulated that someone had dropped an old silver watchcase down the well. I wonder could all those silver dreams possibly have resulted from an old silver watchcase dropped down a well being drilled many years before?

The Facts of Life

Children raised on a farm have always had one advantage over their city cousins. They are frequently faced with life and death and birth situations whether it is with their farm animal or neighbors'. They learn the hard way that too many expectations are not realized for instance; cows usually go off and hide during the birthing process. A child was often sent to hunt them. Most of the time the cow and new calf would be fine but there was always that exception when the cow wasn't fine, when she needed help to expel a dead calf, when she had been too long without help and the child learned that things don't always go right. Life isn't fair!

Sometimes a pregnant ewe delivers twin lambs; she may immediately choose one and butt the other away. The owner will hold the ewe so the lamb can suckle. The ewe may eventually accept her little one but probably not. It may end up in the orphan lamb bunch. I had seven tiny ones in a wooden box beside our wood fireplace, our only source of heat. It wasn't much fun but it had to be done. Life isn't fair!

Perhaps a mink invades the chicken house and all at once future flocks of white Leghorn laying hens are wiped out. Life isn't fair!

These are lessons a farm child learns.

One job entrusted to bigger children was taking a cow to visit a neighbor's bull. The next farm, up the road, had a big polled Hereford bull in residence. Many farmers did not have enough cows to warrant keeping a bull. When one of the cows came into heat, someone would let the cow out of the gate into the road and get her headed in the right direction and up the road they'd go usually at a trot. The bull would be bellowing in anticipation. The neighbor would open a gate and put your cow in the bull lot and you went on to the house out of sight of the proceedings. After you visited with the women folks for a time, someone would come and say, "The cow is ready", and back down the road you went, always with a long switch in your hand in case the cow decided to visit a cornfield beside the road. The price for the cow's visit was $2, payable when a live calf was delivered.

My uncle Harve also had a big Hereford bull, which we could use without charge. There was a problem, however, in order to get to that bull, we had to go across the iron bridge and cows just don't want to walk across a bridge. It took a lot of yelling and threatening by at least two people to persuade the cow to cross. The bull lot was right beside and across the road from their front porch, much to Aunt Arkie's disgust. If she had company on the front porch and someone brought a cow for service, she would have to get up and go inside the house and pretend she didn't know what was going on right there across the road.

I don't know why Uncle Harve put that bull lot there unless it was to aggravate Aunt Arkie. He was good at that! She nagged him from morning to night. Daddy asked him one time, "How could he stand it?" Uncle Harve just grinned and said, "Actually, I kind of enjoy it." I think he did enjoy the constant banter because he deliberately did things to set her off. She was the best housekeeper I've ever known. Sadly, Aunt Arkie died of throat cancer when she was 69. Uncle Harve married a widow, Fanny, and was overheard bragging about how much better she was in the bedroom than his first wife.

The Tragedy of the White Leghorns

I remember waking up one morning to excitement. I remember white splotches in the pasture field out around the chicken house and barn. The grownups were upset and talking loudly. Then I discovered what the white splotches were, chickens! Half gown white leghorn pullets that daddy was raising. Each chicken had had its throat slit, by what? That's what they were talking about. I heard the word mink and the word weasel. The chickens' should have been secure, shut up for the night in the henhouse, but some bloodthirsty animal had found a crevice and made its way in with disastrous results.

This was quite a financial loss during the depression. I can still remember the green field with the widely scattered forty dead white leghorn pullets.

Now, looking back I wonder why they couldn't have been made use of. After all, they had been bled by the mink. It looks like they could have been used for food for several families. In fact, the mink had only slit their throats. That was the only mark on them. The dead chickens were loaded on a one-horse sled and hauled around the church hill to the woods where they were just left. Back then dead farm animals were never buried. They were hauled to an isolated spot for the buzzards and "possums" to dine on.

The raid by a mink on our chicken house created quite a stir in our neighborhood. The news was relayed to everybody on the Citizens party line telephone. Hode Shinn, a next farm neighbor was consulted. Hode was a trapper and knew about wild animals and their habits. I remember he came to view the scene and so did a lot of other people. Hode confirmed what everybody suspected, it was a mink.

After this loss, daddy hired a nephew, one of the Crum boys, Hoyt, who was a carpenter to build a state of the art chicken house. It had three rooms in a row and doors in each end. It was built on a hillside below the barn. This enabled it to have clean out doors below the south facing windows. You could drive a wagon along there and simply rake out the chicken litter. One of the end rooms was used as a feed room. There were 100-pound sacks of laying mash, supposedly the chickens would lay more eggs if they were fed that brand of mash. At first, the feed sacks were plain white soft muslin and they were made into bed sheets, nightgowns, aprons, etc. Eventually someone had a bright idea. The feed started coming in brightly printed colorful designs and you could create everything from kitchen curtains to really nice clothes. You always tried to get at least three sacks alike that you could get a dress pattern cut. I remember making mother and daughter matching dresses for my two daughters and myself in the 1950's. The feed sack material was so soft, it was ideal for children's clothes.

Now printed feed sacks have become collectible. I about fell off my chair when I watched an out of state bidder pay four hundred dollars for a box of twenty printed feed sacks at a local farm auction.

When I was little, we would sometimes taste and compare the different kinds of mash. They weren't bad at all. Our parents would have been horrified and sure we would be sick. Fortunately they never knew!

The Khaki Model T

Cottageville is where we usually did our "storin". That's what I can remember some people calling it when I was little. In the summer this meant a trip in our new Model T Ford. Daddy had never had a car before and he ordered it from Fred Sayre, West Virginia's main Ford dealer. Daddy had always known Fred, actually they were related. One day I was so excited, Fred had called on our Citizens telephone line to say they would be delivering the car that day. I was disappointed when the shiny new car turned into our driveway. Daddy had ordered green and the car was khaki! We thought it was ugly but the official color listed on the car papers was a shade of green. This Model T was a 1927 and the last Model T year. It was the first time you could order a colored car. Henry Ford had been known to say you could have any color you wanted as long as it was black! One thing about it, it was easy to spot in a parking lot. It was the only car of that color I ever saw.

Daddy, who had never been behind the steering wheel of a car before, was given a quick driving lesson by Fred and just turned loose to practice in the pasture field.

We had two horses, Old Charley and his mother, Noble. They, as well as our two cows, came to assess the situation. They soon got bored and wandered off.

I don't know what Daddy would have done if he hadn't had me to help him drive. I was only four but Daddy put me behind the steering wheel where there were two levers. I had to move one when Daddy hollered as he was cranking the engine. Needless to say, I felt very important. I learned that one lever was for spark and the other for gas. After Daddy bought the 1927 Model T for four hundred dollars, he never owned another car. Fred Sayre pestered Daddy every time he saw him, trying to get him to buy another car. Model A's were a better car than the Model T's. I guess

Daddy got tired of Fred and his high pressure selling tactics and avoided him.

Daddy had a garage built out at the big gate that opened into the pasture field. We lived nearly four miles out Cow Run Road which, of course, was a mud road and impassable in winter. Back then you could buy a car license for part of a year since you couldn't drive your car all year if your roads were bad. Anyway, our car was put up on blocks for part of the year. Daddy was not mechanically inclined and I don't think he ever became an expert driver. We were coming down the Ripley Hill and a wheel came off the car, passed us and went merrily rolling on down the hill. I remember another time when we were coming from Ripley, we were always blinded by the afternoon sun and I wished we could go another direction! Daddy picked up a hitchhiker, of course, Daddy always picked up hitchhikers. As a special treat mom usually bought a loaf of baker's bread and bologna to eat when we got home. Now we had crusty brown yeast homemade bread at home. We had country ham too, but we preferred store bought for a change. I was in the back seat with the hitchhiker and mom motioned me to hand her the grocery bag. She unwrapped the bologna and made a big sandwich and gave it to the hitchhiker.

The Khaki Model T became quite well known for Daddy was a one room school teacher and drove the Model T to school and back every day if the roads were passable. Eight different schools in Union District had the benefit of his teaching. He had a lifetime teaching certificate. It lists twelve subjects and the high grade he got in each. One time when I was little, I heard the Jackson County Superintendent of Schools, Clarence Myers tell Daddy that he envied him that lifetime certificate.

I'm afraid back then, in the thirties, politics ruled the school system. Jackson County always went Republican and our family was all staunch Republicans. In spite of the fact that Daddy was known as the best teacher in the district, one year Jackson County went Democratic and Daddy did not get a school that year. Then one year when the Republicans were in power, Avis Baker did not get a school because her uncle, Jake Baker, a Democrat, was always mouthing off with slurs against the Republicans. Avis was a wonderful teacher and she certainly should not have been held responsible for her uncle's remarks but this was Jackson County's dirty politics.